# J.A.H. HUNTER

---

# MATHEMATICAL
# BRAIN-TEASERS

---

DOVER PUBLICATIONS, INC.

NEW YORK

Published in Canada by General Publishing Company, Ltd., 30 Lesmill Road, Don Mills, Toronto, Ontario.
Published in the United Kingdom by Constable and Company, Ltd.

This Dover edition, first published in 1976, is a corrected and enlarged republication of the work originally published by Bantam Books in 1965 under the title *Hunter's Math Brain Teasers*.

*International Standard Book Number: 0-486-23347-2*
*Library of Congress Catalog Card Number: 76-11459*

Manufactured in the United States of America
Dover Publications, Inc.
31 East 2nd Street
Mineola, N.Y. 11501

# PREFACE
## TO THE DOVER EDITION

This Dover edition contains an additional Appendix, E, outlining the Boolean approach that is sometimes useful for solving problems of the "inferential" type (i.e., logic problems). Apart from that, and correction of misprints, there are no changes from the original text.

For the benefit of those who may not be familiar with the popular currency designations that appear in some of the problems here, we note the following: a quarter is 25 cents, a dime 10 cents, a nickel 5 cents.

Toronto, 1976                    J. A. H. HUNTER

# PREFACE

# TO THE FIRST EDITION

More and more people are coming to realize how much fun there can be in the solving of simple little mathematical teasers. If you are one of those fortunate individuals, or are on the way to becoming one, then you may find some diversion in this little collection of problems—mostly quite easy, and none requiring very much mathematical know-how.

That figures *can* be fun seems to be confirmed by the obvious interest taken in such teasers by thousands of kind readers whose encouragement, support, and even ideas have been largely responsible for the publication of this little book.

In thanking those readers, among the many who must remain unnamed, I would like to mention two in particular whose fertile and whimsical brains have been responsible for some of the alphametics that are included here: A. G. Bradbury and Derrick Murdoch.

A note on the text: Appendices A and B are intended to refresh the reader's memory. Appendices C and D offer only a brief outline of what may be quite new concepts to many readers, concepts discussed in detail and at length in textbooks. And finally, the more difficult problems are indicated by asterisks.

So now let's "figure for fun"!

J. A. H. HUNTER

January 1965

# CONTENTS

# CONTENTS

# PROBLEMS

## 1 THE DELUGE

The animals went in two by two,
But some came out by scores.
For little ones born inside the Ark
Came also through its doors.

The rabbits, the rats, the mice, and cats
Had multiplied indeed.
Cooped up in the hulk for ten long months,
What else to do but breed?

For every two beasts that first went in,
There came out twenty-three:
An average, of course, for all the pairs
In that menagerie.

But some of the beasts, the elephants
And other mammals too,
Came out of the Ark as they'd gone in:
Still two by two by two.

The rest of the horde, a seething mob,
Three hundred pairs all told,
Had bred in the Ark and so came forth
Increased just fifteen-fold.

Imagine that scene on Ararat
For Noah and all his kin,
As the animals fanned across the land!
How many beasts went in?

## 2 RIGHT ON THE DOT

Joan glanced at her watch as the little red car pulled in to the curb where she waited. "Right on time!" she told her husband, swinging open the door. "I'll bet you speeded."

Wes shook his head. "You lose." He chuckled. "I just started at the right time. If I'd averaged six miles an hour faster I'd have been five minutes early, but at five miles an hour slower I'd have been six minutes late."

There's a driver for you! How far had he driven?

## 3 THE LUCKY FIND

Jill's father looked at the money on the table. "You've got quite a lot there," he remarked.

"I found two dollars on the sidewalk," the child explained.

"You were lucky." Her father laughed. "Now you've got just five times as much as you'd have had if you'd lost two bucks."

How much did Jill have before her lucky find?

## 4 A POOR EXCUSE

"I want to call Joan," said Celia. "Let's see your little book."

Ken grinned. "You need a better excuse than that, but I'll give you her number."

"Okay, then." Celia picked up the receiver. "You've got a good memory when it suits you."

"It's an easy one," declared her husband. "Shift the first figure and put it after the other three; that gives you one more than three-quarters of her number."

That was easy, of course! What was the number?

## 5 WHAT'S A QUARTER?

"I got your envelopes, Mom," said Dick, putting a paper bag on the table. "Some are air-mail, as you wanted."

"That's fine," his mother told him. "What did you pay?"

"Seventy-two cents for the lot," replied the boy. "The air-mail cost just a quarter more than the others."

What did the air-mail envelopes cost?

## 6 A LONG WAIT

They'd been standing in line quite a while outside the theatre, and Paul was bored. "Here's a job for you," his father said. "Say the first in the line is number one, the second number two, and so on. Figure out the total of all those numbers for all the people ahead of us."

After some busy minutes up and down the line with pencil and paper, Paul came back to report.

"There's exactly a third as many kids as grown-ups," he declared. "But it's funny that the grown-ups' numbers come to three times what the kids' numbers do."

"What's the total then?" his father asked.

"Between eight hundred and a thousand," replied the boy.

So you'll have to take it from there too!

## 7 WHO CHECKS THE CHECKS?

"Separate checks, please," Joe told the waitress. "Sam had as many coffees as the total number of items Ted and I have each consumed."

The girl handed each his own check. "It still comes to one dollar and five cents for each of you," she said. "One check would have done."

"Quite a coincidence then," chuckled Sam. "We all had coffee, pie, and ice cream and nothing else. But different numbers of ice creams, and Ted ate the most."

It was certainly odd the way those checks came out. Coffee was a dime a cup, ice creams were twenty cents each, and pie fifteen cents a piece.

What exactly had each of them had?

## 8 THE TRUTH WILL OUT

One experience when over in Kalota last fall really had me puzzled.

You know that odd custom in the island? Men always tell the truth. A woman, however, never makes two consecutive true or untrue statements: if one is true, her next is a lie, and vice versa. And the same goes for the boys and the girls.

Meeting a Kalotan couple with their child, I asked the kid: "Are you a boy?"

The reply was in Kalotan!

Fortunately, the parents both spoke our language. "Kibi said, 'I am a boy'," one of them declared. "Kibi is a girl. Kibi lied," the other parent told me.

Well! What can you make of that?

## 9 COCKTAILS*

"Cocktails:" said the invitations, "six to eight." But it was after nine when the first half-dozen guests departed, and an hour later when the last diehard left.

Judy sighed, surveying the litter of glasses. "Now we can have a bite at last," she said. "But the caviar crackers are all gone."

"I didn't eat either." Tony chuckled. "Fanny sure likes caviar: she had a third as many of them as the rest of the guests would have eaten if they'd consumed one more altogether than they did."

Fanny—that's Miss Filltum, of course—is lots of fun, and they both like her. But she had killed those tasty crackers! Her performance had brought the average consumption of them up to one more per head than the average for all the other guests.

How many guests had there been?

## 10 A MATTER OF WEIGHT

"What's the weight of this one?" asked Mrs Pothersniff, pointing to a large crab there on the wet slab.

Fred considered the question a moment. He had to have his little joke, and Fred was no respecter of persons. "It weighs exactly three-quarters of its weight, and three-quarters of three-quarters of a pound," he told the pompous customer. "I guess you'll want it dressed."

The lady wasn't amused! But what did the crab weigh?

## 11 BY CANDLELIGHT

They had dined restfully by candlelight, and now Celia was sewing while Jim relaxed doing nothing in particular.

"We never blew out those candles," he said suddenly. "Look at them. One's exactly twice as long as the other."

Celia looked. "That's funny," she told him. "You lit them when we started dinner, and they were new and the same length. They're from that lot you got before Christmas."

"That explains it." Her husband laughed. "I

bought two different sorts. One was guaranteed to burn for six hours, but the other for only four."

How long had those two candles been burning?


## 12 HOW RED ARE THE ROSES!

It was their first house, with all the fun of planning their very first garden.

"The roses will go there," said Sally, pointing to the sketch she'd made. "Rows and rows of them, with the same number in each."

"I mailed the order today," Bill told her. "Close to a hundred bucks on roses alone, so they'd better look good."

His wife smiled. "You won't get away with that. It was well under a hundred bucks," she declared. "I had planned for eight rows, but now I realize we'll be one short for that."

Bill jotted down some figures. "You'd be three short if you had seven rows but exactly right for nine rows."

They should have a fine display with all those roses at thirty-six cents a bush. How many did Bill order?


## 13 TWO BOYS AND A GIRL

When Ted was twice
    as old as Sue,
Her brother Clive
    was twenty-two.
When Sue was twice
    as old as Clive,
Then Ted himself
    was twenty-five.
Their ages total
    one nought three,
So now what must
    their ages be?

## 14 A MAGIC SQUARE

"Magic squares" have intrigued people for thousands of years.

The simplest "magic square," which was known to the ancient Chinese at least three thousand years ago, used the nine numerals as shown in this diagram:

| 8 | 3 | 4 |
|---|---|---|
| 1 | 5 | 9 |
| 6 | 7 | 2 |

This is called a "magic square" because all rows and columns, and the two main diagonals as well, add up to the same total: in this case 15, which is the "magic constant" of this example.

It is not an essential condition, however, for the numbers in a "magic square" to be consecutive.

We now show the outline of a different nine-number "magic square," with only two of the individual numbers filled in: 7 and 13. For this "magic square" the "magic constant" is 111, and you have to fill in the other seven numbers.

|    |   | 7 |
|----|---|---|
| 13 |   |   |
|    |   |   |

## 15 FIVE SECONDS FOR THIS!

"That's a nice cup," Doug commented, spooning sugar into his coffee. "A pretty contrast to the color of the saucer. Did you get these today?"

"Just the cup and saucer. Fancy you noticing!" Ann laughed. "I chose them separately, and the cup cost a dollar more than the saucer. One dollar fifty for the two, so don't say I waste money."

How much was the cup alone? Quick, now!

## 16 SO LONG AGO

Susan looked up from the little book. "It's an old diary," she said. "I've been reading what I wrote in it one very special last day of a month. The day we first met."

But Sam wasn't going to be drawn. "Special? I'd say unique," he told her, turning down the radio. "If you add the number of previous days in that month to the excess of long months over short months for the other months of the year, you get the number of days in the month that followed the month we first met."

He thought a moment. "And that special day of the month was the sum of the two halves of that year's date, the first half and the second half."

Susan was well accustomed to her husband's teasing. But what was the exact date of that entry in her diary?

## 17 FUN FOR A FISHERMAN

Bill signed the check and slipped it into the envelope with his letter. "If they're like the ad says," he commented, "Pete should have fine fishing this trip."

His wife picked up the magazine and studied the advertisement he had marked. "They only show the four lures," she said. "Spinners down to spoons. But what a price range! A dollar thirty-nine, a dollar and four cents, eighty-three cents, and fifty-nine cents."

"I ordered a selection of all four," Bill told her. "Twelve lures for exactly twelve dollars."

How many had he ordered at each price?

## 18 A REAL TWISTER

If my three were a four
And my one were a three,
What I am would be nine
Less than half what I'd be.

I'm only three digits,
Just three in a row.
So what in the world
Must I be? Do you know?

## 19 FOUR APPLES APIECE

"You didn't tell me you were going," cried Sally, as her two brothers came in with their apples. "I wanted some too."

Paul put his bag on the table. "Okay, you'll have your share," he told her. "Jim got five and I got seven, so we can have four each."

"And they'll cost you twelve cents in all, the same as the price we paid," added Jim.

How did the boys apportion that twelve cents?

## 20 ONE AMONG TWELVE

"I'm just a penny short of half a dollar," said Peter, checking his twelve coins on the table.

"That's funny," his sister told him. "I'm exactly

the same, and with twelve coins too. But you've got one coin I haven't got."

What coins did each have?

## 21 HOW OLD WAS ANNIE?

"How old am I?"

Aunt Annie said.

"Well, now just let us see.

"My present age

is five times what

"It five years hence will be,

"Less five times what

it was five years

"Ago, you will agree."

## 22 WHEN SPRING WAS NEAR*

"Did you order the bulbs?" asked Helen. "I saw you checked three lots on that ad last night."

Bob nodded. "Those are what I ordered. Ten daffodils for a dollar ninety-eight and two sorts of tulips—twenty-five for a dollar forty-eight and twenty-five for a dollar ninety-eight."

"They give a bonus of twelve snowdrop bulbs with each lot." Helen misses no bargains! "How many lots did you send for?"

"I just can't remember." Her husband frowned. "Complete lots, of course, and I do know we get eight hundred and eighty bulbs altogether for our forty dollars."

They'd have a gay display in the spring. What exactly did Bob order?

## 23 BE CAREFUL NOW!

Tom was playing with the power drill he'd given his son for Christmas, when the boy came in.

"Could you bore a five-inch hole with that, Dad?" Ken asked. "I mean diameter."

"Not with this drill," Tom told him. "It would be a big hole."

The boy nodded. "That's what I thought," he said. "But teacher asked how deep the hole would be if we drilled it centrally through a solid ball thirteen inches in diameter."

Ken's teacher must have meant a true spherical ball. So how deep would the hole be?

## 24 HOW FAR? HOW FAR?

They had walked steadily for twenty-seven minutes since leaving the cottage, and Jeff was weary already. "How far have we come, Dad?" he asked plaintively.

Wes smiled. "Half as far as we are from Tulla. It's right on our road to Dill, so we can stop for a drink there."

Eight miles further along their route, Jeff stopped. "I'm beat," he moaned. "How far are we still from Dill?"

"Not too far now," Wes told him. "Just half as far as we are from Tulla."

Fifty years ago it would have seemed only a short stroll. But how far did they have to walk from the cottage to Dill?

## 25 HIS FIRST JOB

It isn't a great job, but Bob knows he's lucky to have work at all just now.

If he earned one cent more in three hours than he would earn in five hours if he earned twice as much in seven hours as he earns in four hours, his hourly rate would be seventy cents more than it is.

Bob hopes to reach that within a year, but what is the boy's present rate?

## 26 JINGLE, JINGLE

Mary started laughing when Bert came in. "You jingle as you walk," she told him.

"Sure I do," he retorted. "My pants pockets are full of the Community Chest cash we collected in the office. Something under twenty bucks, all in dimes and quarters."

"Pockets don't sound very safe," his wife said. "I suppose you know how much."

"The same amount in each pocket." Bert chuckled. "In the left pocket I've got the same number of each, but in the right side pocket there's as much in quarters as there is in dimes."

So he knew! Can you figure out the exact total?

## 27 THE THIRSTY HUNTERS

We can't reveal the full story of this shocking incident, but the main facts can be recorded.

Two hunters, still thirsty after a long day in the woods, wanted to share their last bottle of rye. They contrived to divide the twenty-four ounces of liquor exactly equally, and with only seven distinct transfers from container to container, although they had only that bottle and two other containers, an eleven-ounce and a five-ounce measure.

How did they manage to do it?

## 28 JELLY BEANS

Walt waited while the crowd of children made their purchases. When the little store was quiet once more, he turned to his old friend behind the counter. "Those jelly beans seem a good line," he commented. "The kids were all going for them."

Sam smiled. "I guess they're good value at four cents an ounce," he said. "And it's odd the way the price worked out with that last lot of sales. Dollar for pound and cent for ounce, I took the same as the total weight sold."

What weight of jelly beans had he sold?

## 29 THE INSURANCE AGENT

"So you're just forty," said Bill, flipping the pages of his rate book. "With three kids, eh? How old are they?"

"Lay off. You're not insuring them too." Bert laughed. "But figure it out yourself. Their three ages add up to the number of this house, and multiplied together they make my age."

Bill thought hard. "I get what you mean, but I still can't tell their ages for sure."

"Forget it then," Bert told him, glancing at his watch. "The two older kids will be walking back from school now, so you'll meet them."

That was all Bill needed to know, and he gave the three ages without further delay.

What were they?

## 30 DON'T SNEEZE NOW*

Ted paused in his dealing. He sneezed violently, and some of the cards in his hand fell to the floor. "There goes my luck!" he exclaimed.

But Sam looked under the table. "All face down, so pick them up and carry on," he said. "Anyway, you dropped only one less than you've dealt to my partner and myself together."

Bob laughed. "That's right," he agreed. "And

you've still got just three times as many undealt cards in your hand as you've dealt me."

Len didn't object, so Ted picked up the fallen cards and went on dealing.

It was a friendly game of bridge, but how many cards had he dropped?

### 31 UP IN SMOKE

"You've left only half,
    you bad lad!"
Ted's father was really
    quite mad.
"You've smoked up
    the square
"Of a third of
    what's there."
How many cigars
    had Dad had?

### 32 LATE OR EARLY?

"What time did you come in last night?" her mother asked, when Ann appeared for breakfast. "Must have been late."

The girl shook her head. "Early," she said. "The minute hand was exactly on the minute one minute ahead of the hour hand."

Without looking at your watch, can you figure out what time Ann returned?

### 33 WHAT STAMPS?*

The clerk picked up the dimes Jill had put on the counter. "But what stamps do you want?" he asked.

The little girl looked unhappy. "Dad wants one-cent, two-cent, three-cent, five-cent, and ten-cent," she replied. "He said to get four each of two sorts and three each of the others, but I've forgotten which."

Postal clerks have to handle tougher problems than that. "I guess he gave you the exact money for them," he told her. "Just these dimes."

What stamps did Jill have to buy?

## 34 A CLOSE SECRET

"My age?" she smiled.
"You'll have to guess.
"Just let me think.
"Ah, that's it: yes."

"Reverse my age:
"Divide by three:
"Add thirty-four.
"My age you'll see."

That's what she said.
So can you say
How old she must
Have been that day?

## 35 A MATTER OF IFS

If Sam had driven for twenty minutes less than the time he would have driven if he had driven twenty miles less than he did drive but at two-thirds the speed at which he drove, he would have driven ten miles less than he did.

If he had driven twenty minutes longer than the time he would have driven if he had driven ten miles less than he did drive but at three-quarters the speed at which he drove, he would have driven twenty miles further.

No more "ifs"! But how far did Sam drive?

## 36 SEVEN LESS, SEVEN MORE

"I saw your boy last night," said Charlie. "Hadn't seen him in years. How old is he now?"

Tom smiled. "Ted's not as old as he makes out to be," he replied. "Seven years ago he was a third as old as me, and in seven years' time I'll be twice his age."

That told Charlie all he wanted to know.

So how old was Tom?

## 37 A LEGAL LUMINARY

"Why wasn't I a lawyer?" Ted laughed, eyeing the skis his friend was strapping on the car. "You get the breaks."

"But I work hard when I am working," Bill told him. "Last month I averaged fourteen hours a day the days I worked."

Ted shook his head. "You won't convince me," he said. "How many hours a day did you average over the whole month?"

Bill had expected something like that. "Exactly nine, and including Sundays," he replied.

How many days had Bill worked the previous month?

## 38 BUTTONS AND BUTTONS

"I've sorted these buttons," Sally declared. "There are six lots, each a different shade."

Her mother looked. "Only two different colors, blues and reds," she commented. "You matched the shades nicely."

Sally nodded. "That's all there were, and each lot's a different number: five, six, twelve, fourteen, twenty-three, and twenty-nine."

Her mother took one lot of the buttons. "I can

use these right now, she said. "That leaves twice as many reds and blues."

How many did she take?

## 39 THE MORTICIANS' BANQUET

"You sure had a party," commented Linda, when her husband came home from the morticians' banquet. "Were there many there?"

"Not too many," John told her, swaying slightly as he stood. "In fact, we were seven less than twice the product of the two digits of our total number."

Linda didn't quite see what the fingers of the revellers had to do with it! But she was sleepy anyway.

How many had attended that dinner?

## 40 WHEN LEGS WERE FOR WALKING

"It's near ten, Dad," said Sam. "You'd best get going, and I'll follow when I'm through."

"Okay." His father made for the door. "Three miles an hour is my speed, and it's quite a step to Jake's place."

But Sam was through sooner than he had expected, and he set off just half an hour after his father. And after one hour's brisk walk, he came to Hank's cottage. "Stop in for a drink," called Hank. "Your Dad passed five minutes ago but wouldn't stop."

It was tempting! "Thank you kindly. I guess I will," replied Sam, after a moment's thought. "I can stay thirty-five minutes and still catch him just as he reaches Jake's farm if I walk the same speed as I've been doing."

That was long ago! But how far was it altogether to Jake's place?

## 41 NO MORE STICKS

Here are nine matches.
Without breaking or bending, you have to re-arrange them so as to make three squares.
You have only the nine sticks.

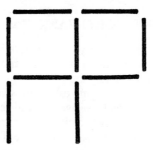

## 42 THE CROCODILE

That croc was a freak,
    not at all the right shape,
With a tail thrice as long
        as its head.
Its body was short,
    far too short for the rest;
Half as long as its tail,
        so they said.

The body and tail
    measured thirteen feet six:
An ugly great brute,
        you'll agree.
But I never discovered
    the length of its head.
Just how long do you think
        it would be?

## 43 IT GOES SO FAST

Jill looked at the dimes in her brother's hand. "Is that all you have left?" she asked. "You had almost a dollar this morning."

"I spent the rest," Jack told her. "Half of what I spent is two-thirds of what I've got."

How much had he spent?

## 44 A DOG AND HIS KENNEL

"Is that right, you paid more than twenty bucks for him?" asked Rod, peering over the fence.

Bert grinned. "That's with his kennel too," he said. "If the pooch had cost five dollars more, the kennel would have been a third of the total. If the kennel had been five bucks less, I'd have spent three-quarters of the total on the dog."

That kept Rod quiet for a while!

What had the dog cost Bert?

## 45 THE WINDOW

They were playing out in my back yard when the crash of broken glass took me out on the run. And there I found the four children viewing the debris of the garage window, obviously shattered by one of them.

"John did it," said Ann.

John grinned. "It was Gail broke it," he assured me.

"Anyway, it wasn't me," his sister Sally declared.

Gail was the picture of innocence. "Me?" she exclaimed. "John's a liar when he says I did it."

Only one of them had spoken the truth, so who was the culprit?

## 46 SO MANY COINS

Uncle Ken opened the money box and peered inside. "You've got seventy coins here," he told Kim. "D'you know how much it is?"

"Just eighty-three cents short of two dollars," his nephew replied hopefully, "and it's all in pennies, nickels, and dimes."

"You figure out how many dimes there must be," Uncle Ken told him. "Then I might make it up to two bucks."

It may have been a lucky guess, but Kim did it. Can you?

## 47 WATCH THOSE PENNIES

"What did you pay for the pears?" asked Betty, always suspicious when her husband does the shopping.

"I did notice the price," Doug replied. "They charged me at the rate of a dime for three."

"Too much," Betty commented. "I bought just as many of the same pears as those on Monday, but they were at a quarter for eight."

Her husband laughed. "You sure watch the pennies," he said. "There's only a nickel difference between what we paid." How many pears had each of them bought?

## 48 WHAT IS THIS?

Take half of this,
          and add one more.
Then treble that,
          and add on four.

But just the same
          result you'd see,

By adding this
  to twenty-three.

So what is "this"?
    You'll have to say!
Your fun with figures
    for today.


## 49 ALL IN A FAMILY

"Relationships are funny," remarked Bob. "Tom's the same relation to you that I am to your son."

"So he is." Charlie chuckled. "And you're the same relation to me that Tom is to you."

What relation was Charlie to Tom?


## 50 SIZE AND SIDES

"Your picture frame's ready," said Sam. "Maybe you'd like to look before I wrap it."

The narrow black molding certainly looked good with its fine gold inset, but something was wrong. Steve grabbed a ruler and checked.

"This side's six inches longer than two-thirds the length I wanted," he cried. "And that side should have been six inches longer than three-quarters of what you've made it."

"But it's exactly twenty inches square," Sam protested.

Steve shook his head. "That's what's wrong!" he told him.

What dimensions had Steve wanted for the frame?

### 51 A LOT OF TILES*

"Well, what d'you think of them?" asked Joe, pointing to the four tables, each with its square top newly surfaced in tiny square tiles. "I just finished the job."

Ted examined his friend's handiwork. "Very neat," he said. "I see each top has six fewer tiles to the side than the next larger one."

"That's right, and all the tiles are identical," Joe replied. "They were the complete top of a hideous old relic. It was square too, and luckily all the tiles were there and I didn't break any."

Having just the right number was quite a coincidence. How many was that?

### 52 NO FUN FOR HER*

"That's the last social chore I do for you." Ann hurled her hat into a far corner of the room as she came in. "Such a bunch of bores! Over a hundred of them, and more women than men at that."

Doug grinned, guessing what he'd missed. "Sorry," he replied contritely. "How many men were at the party?"

Ann smiled maliciously. "Twice as many men as there would have been women if *kaazi* of the women had been men and if half-*kaazi* of the remaining women had not been there at all," she told her husband. "There were eleven women more than there would have been if a third of the men had been women and half the women had been men."

*Kaazi* is a Kalotan word, a particular whole number in the language of that exotic island. What is that number?

### 53 FIGURING IN KALOTA

If five times eight
    makes 44,

And six times five
            makes 33,
Then what, by this
            Kalotan law,
Would four times five
            times seven be?

## 54 ONE HONEST MAN

"The knives are forty-nine cents each, and the forks thirty-nine," said the girl. "So they're five dollars and a quarter altogether."

But Mike had figured it out in his head. "You'd be robbing yourself of two cents," he told her, chuckling. And he was right.

How many of each had Mike bought?

## 55 WHEN AGE MATTERS

"When I was as old as you were when I was two years younger than I am now," Jack told his sister, "you were a third as old as I'll be in two years' time."

Jill digested this piece of information, her fingers figuring fast. "You're smart," she replied. "When I'm as old as you were when I was three years older than you were when you were twice as old as I was, you'll be just a year older than you are."

How old were they?

## 56 NO PEEKING AT WATCHES

"What's the time?" asked Willie, winding his watch. "I've never known an afternoon drag so slowly."

Ted turned his wrist. "At the next minute, it'll be exactly twice as many seconds after the half-hour as it was minutes before the same half-hour last

time the two hands were at right angles this afternoon."

No peeking now! What would the time be?

## 57 THE SOUND OF CASH*

"Who wants cash?" asked Uncle Fred, chinking
the coins in his clenched fists as he came into the
room.

"Me!" "Me!" cried Jack and Jill, grabbing at his
hands. But their uncle was ready. "If the pennies
in my left hand were dimes and the nickels in my
right hand pennies, I'd have one dollar more," he
told them. "If the nickels in my right hand were
dimes and the pennies in my left hand nickels,
I'd have twice as much altogether."

He repeated his words slowly and then added,
"That would not be possible if I had even one coin
less."

Just what coins did he have altogether in his
hands?

## 58 CHECK YOUR CHECKERBOARD

Imagine you have removed one or other pair of
diagonally opposite corner squares from a checkerboard.

A lot of imagination is needed, for now you have
to imagine that you have an ample supply of
regular dominoes so big that each tile will exactly
cover two squares of your checkerboard—placed
up and down or across the board.

How many of those dominoes are required,
placed in that way, if all the remaining squares of
your checkerboard are to be covered?

## 59 ASSORTED SOCKS

"So you bought yourself a dozen pairs of socks," said Mary. "That cost you plenty."

Her husband smiled. "Only twelve bucks," he told her. "The thick ones were cheap, fifty cents a pair. Then I got some at a dollar fifty, and some at two dollars a pair."

How many had he bought at each price?

## 60 THOSE XMAS CARDS*

Joan bought her Christmas cards early last year: no last minute rush, with all the best ones gone. Having picked what she wanted, she handed the clerk the thirty cards. "I'll have these, please."

The young man found envelopes and then checked the prices. "A dime, fifteen cents," he muttered, reading the price tags, "forty cents, a quarter."

"That's right," agreed Joan. "Five each of two designs, and ten each of the other two." She put some one dollar bills on the counter. "There's the exact money, and I don't want a receipt."

There aren't many customers like that! What had those cards cost her?

## 61 LET'S BE OLD-FASHIONED

When first the marriage knot was tied
Between my wife and me,
My age did hers as much exceed
As three times three does three.

When six good years and half six years
We man and wife had been,
Her age to mine compared the same
As twelve to just fourteen.

How old d'you make the two of us?
You'll do it in your head.
How old d'you say we must have been
The happy day we wed?


## 62 ONE GAINS, ONE LOSES

"That's a fine clock," Doug remarked, admiring
the modern timepiece on the buffet.

"Electric, and it keeps perfect time." Steve glanced
at his watch. "I set my watch by it at noon today,
but my watch gains just a minute an hour."

"That's better than mine," declared Doug. "I set
my watch by the radio time signal at noon today,
and it loses two minutes an hour."

Steve's mind was working fast. "The clock's exactly on a minute mark," he said. "So my watch
must be showing twice as much after the hour as
yours showed after the hour an hour ago."

Obviously both watches needed fixing. But what
was the right time?


## 63 GRADE 7

"So you teach arithmetic," commented Alan.
"You don't look the type at all."

"I don't quite know how to take that," said
Betty. "We have fun with it."

Alan laughed. "That explains it then. How many
in your class?"

The girl thought a moment. "You figure it out,"
she replied. "A third of them are under twelve,
half of them are under thirteen, and six are under
eleven years old. There are as many between eleven
and twelve as there are between twelve and thirteen."

Now *you* figure it out!

## 64 THE SECRET IS OUT!

It's Sally's birthday tomorrow, but maybe she won't want to be reminded of it. It's too bad the way those years catch up with a girl!

If she were only ten years younger then she'd be a year younger tomorrow than half as old as she'd be if she were only four years younger than three times as old as her boy friend was when he was three years older than half as old as she was on her last birthday.

So now you know how old Sally will be tomorrow.

## 65 A TALE OF TILES

"I plan to tile that wall in the bathroom," said Doug. "Pink and red."

"Should be pretty!" Ann was tactful. "You mean a pattern?"

"All pink in the middle, with a wide border of red tiles all round," replied her husband, checking the figuring he'd been doing. "I'll make that border the same width top, bottom, and sides, with as many tiles in it as there'll be in the pink middle."

Ann peeped over his shoulder. "So you've got it all measured up," she commented. "Exactly eight feet by fifteen."

"That's right," agreed Doug. "The square tiles I want come in three sizes: three-inch, four-inch, and five-inch. They must all be the same size, and I'm figuring out which size to get."

Maybe you can solve his problem.

## 66 A LUCKY BREAK*

Bob smiled as his secretary came into the room. "I'm through now, Fran," he told her. "Please call in the others."

A few moments later they had all assembled—
all four of them, including Frances—and were standing before their boss. But Bob quickly put them at
their ease. "Good news," he said. "The Dunster
deal's through, so here's a bonus of two hundred
thirty dollars to be distributed among the four of
you."

Handing each an envelope, Bob went on. "I've
figured it out exactly in proportion to completed
years you've each been with me, but allowing half
as much again for a man as for a girl."

It was a happy surprise for them, their completed
"years of service" being two, five, six, and seven.
But you'll have to figure out the details.

## 67 LIKE A PARADOX

"Look, Dad." Paul pointed to the paper on which
he'd been figuring. "Four years ago I was twice as
old as Hettie."

His father looked. "So what?" he asked. "Nothing
very odd about that."

"But there is," said the boy. "I'm older now,
yet I'm only half again as old as she is."

How old was he?

## 68 THERE'S NO LOGIC IN THIS

Don't blame the author if this keeps you from
your bed!

Write down the nine digits, 1 through 9, in their
regular order, preferably with spaces between them.
Then write in two plus signs and two minus signs,
so that the resulting expression equals 100.

For example, if you had to make up 24 using
only the first three digits and one plus sign, you
could have $1 + 23 = 24$.

## 69 A MATTER OF AGES

"When Gwen is twice
                as old as Dean,
"Then I shall be
                just seventeen.
"But Gwendoline
                was twenty-three,
"When Dean was twice
                as old as me."
That's what Bill said.
                So tell us, then,
How old he was
                when Dean was ten.

## 70 IT'S A HABIT!

"Take the lot," said Sam, throwing a pack of cigarettes across the office as Ted and Joe came in. "I gave it up at midnight last night."

Joe gave Ted a friendly shove. "Great minds!" he chuckled. "That's just what we've both done too."

So three days passed, and then some more. And one Monday morning Ted was seen to light a cigarette. "My first," he declared, "and one a day won't hurt me."

One became two—you know how it is—and the next to succumb was Sam one dismal Tuesday. He had at least abstained just half as long again as Ted.

Joe held out for more than a month, the only one of the trio to do so. But there came a Wednesday when he also fell. "I stuck it exactly twice as long as you did, Ted," he said. "And I'd still be pure if you guys hadn't cracked."

A good excuse, maybe! But how many days had Joe held out?

## 71 AT THE SUMMER COTTAGE

"You were out early," said Jim, as his son came in for breakfast. "Trying the new boat?"

Ron nodded. "It was too dark when I arrived last night." He gulped his coffee. "I took her over the bay to Dill and turned Ted out, and then we crossed the lake to Penn Point and roused Len."

"So you won't be ashore much today." His father laughed. "It'll be good and hot out there."

"A scorcher," agreed Ron. "Going over to Len the sun near blinded me as I held her on course for the old mill by his cottage."

"Well, watch for that rock just halfway between Penn Point and Dill," Tom reminded him, recalling many narrow escapes.

"I'm a navigator," the boy boasted. "The rock's as far from our dock as it is from Penn Point."

His course had been due north across the bay to Dill. What would it have been direct to Len's place?

## 72 AT THE MIDWAY*

"No more midways for me," said Bill. "I hadn't been in years, so I went last night. It cost me the best part of ten bucks for the booths I went into."

"That's a lot," commented Mike. "Prices must have gone up."

"Maybe," replied Bill. "I had to pay a dime to go into each booth. And then it happened that in each of them I spent just one cent less than half the cash I had left. I came out of the last with exactly seven cents in my pocket."

"I guess you had your fun," Mike told him. "How many did you go into then?"

Do you know?

## 73 COUNT THE HEADS

"Dad, I want some guinea pigs," said Tom. "Larry showed me his today, and he's got parakeets too."

"Quite a zoo!" commented his father. "How many does he have then?"

"They've got fifteen heads and fifty legs," replied the boy.

How many guinea pigs did Larry have?

## 74 THE NURSERY DRAPES

"I bought two lovely materials for the nursery drapes," said Molly. "Real bargains in the sale."

"They'd better be!" Jim smiled. "What did you pay?"

"Less than ten dollars, so don't worry," replied his wife. "I got as many yards of each as its price per yard in cents, and paid two dollars and fifteen cents more for one than the other."

How many yards of each had she bought?

## 75 QUITE A GIRL!

We know a young
          chick in Dundee,
Whose age has its
          last digit "three."
The square
          of the first
Is her whole
          age reversed.
So what must the
          lady's age be?

## 76 A LONG, LONG LEASE

"I'm sorry about so many coins this week," said
Len, handing over his rent money. "But the total's
right: an exact amount in dollars as usual."

"That's what matters." Mr. Kemnitz chuckled.
"You can pay it all in quarters so far as I'm concerned."

Len thought a moment. "You've given me an
idea," he told his landlord. "What say I pay in
one-dollar bills, quarters, and half-dollars in future:
any or all of just those three? And I'll make it a
different combination every week and never repeat."

Mr. Kemnitz smiled. "Okay with me," he declared.
"But you'd have to repeat after nearly nine years
—anyway, more than eight—and I can't guarantee
to keep the rent what it is all that time."

It was all a joke, of course. But what was the
amount of Len's weekly rent?

## 77 OUTSIDE THE THEATRE

They were none of them in a good mood standing at the end of the long line. "Don't forget, you
buy your own tickets today," said Helen. "You'd
better have enough."

Jack watched sulkily as Jill checked her cash.
"I've got three-quarters of a dollar and three-quarters
of what Jill has," he told his mother. "And Jill's
got half a dollar and half of what I have."

That was plenty for the show. But how much
did each of the children have?

## 78 WHAT THE DRAFTSMAN MISSED

A blueprint often shows three different views of
an object: the front elevation, which is the view
from the front; the side elevation, the view from the
side at right angles to the front elevation; and

the plan view, "looking down" at right angles to the other two views.

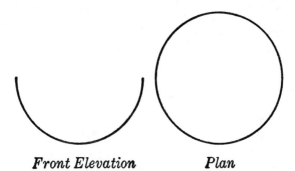

*Front Elevation*          *Plan*

Here we have shown the front elevation and plan view of a certain object, but without the side elevation. Can you draw the missing side elevation and identify what this object could possibly be?

## 79 MOM'S THE BANKER

Pete was persistent. "But I haven't a cent left," he insisted.

His mother smiled. "Okay," she told him, handing over some cash. "But you'll get no more this month. You've borrowed well into next month's pocket money already."

The boy checked the amount happily. "Thanks, Mom," he said. "That gives me a dime a day and an extra two dimes Saturdays, or twelve cents every day right through to the end of the month."

How much had his mother given him?

## 80 SOME RIGHT, SOME WRONG

"How did you both do in the exam?" asked Walt, when the children came home.

"Not so good," replied Ann. "I got a third of the answers wrong."

"It was tough," Bill told his father. "I got five of them wrong, but between us two we answered three-quarters of the questions right."

How many did Ann answer correctly?

## 81 YOU CAN'T SPLIT A PENNY

"How much have you got?" Jill asked hopefully.

Jack delved deep in his pockets. "If I had a quarter more and also a dollar, I'd have twice as much as I'd have if I had only three-quarters of what I've got," he replied.

Jill thought a moment. "Could you have that three-quarters?" she asked.

"Sure," replied Jack. And that told her all she wanted to know.

How much did Jack have?

## 82 THE CIRCULAR LAWN*

"So you've got your circular lawn done," said Doug, admiring the lush green growth. "What's the idea of the three little pegs on the edge?"

"For figuring out the circumference," Mike told him. "It's a true circle. This peg is thirty-five feet from that one and thirty-nine feet from the third across the lawn, and those two are precisely ten feet from each other."

He pointed to a heap of big tiles nearby. "They're exactly one foot square. They'll just fit in comfortably all the way round, edge to edge, as a protection for the grass."

Doug refrained from commenting on his friend's rather odd method. But how many tiles would be used?

## 83 THE NEW TELLER

"There's a new girl at the bank, and she wouldn't cash your check at first," said Simple Simon, putting some money on the table. "That's what she gave me, all but thirty-five cents I spent on a book."

His mother gasped, checking the cash. "She won't stay long," she told the boy. "You've brought me back exactly twice as much as she should have given you."

Banks provide for such little mistakes, but that new teller had really made a mix-up. She'd paid out dollars for cents and cents for dollars!

What was the actual amount of the check?

## 84 NO MINIMUM WAGE

If Peter earned as many cents an hour as the number of dollars Pam would earn in four weeks if Pam earned as many cents each week as Peter earns in forty hours, Peter would earn eighty-seven cents an hour more than he does.

What is Peter's hourly rate?

## 85 THE PECULIAR PAINTERS

"We got through a lot today," said Alan, wiping the paint off his hands. "What's left for tomorrow should take us only an hour longer than what we did today. That's if we work at just the same speeds."

"That's right," agreed Ben. "It's funny, but the number to be done tomorrow will have the same figures as what we did today but the other way round."

Alan nodded. "You mean in reverse order. And it's also funny that the first figure of today's total is the number you paint per hour, while the other figure is my hourly rate."

Indeed, a strange pair to be painting trays! But how many had they painted that day?

## 86 HOW MANY EGGS?

"I got your eggs," said Ron, back home from school. "They're in the kitchen, seventy-two cents' worth."

"That's fine, dear," replied his mother. "How many did you buy?"

The boy grinned. "You say," he told her. "If I'd got just two more for the money, they would have cost six cents a dozen less."

Now *you* say!

## 87 A MATTER OF ODDS

"It's odd the way luck goes," said Wes, toying with a die he'd found tucked away in the table drawer after their game. "I've always been lucky with dice, but not cards."

"Okay, I'll take you up on that," Doug told him. "We'll each have one throw and I'll bet you a dollar I throw higher than you."

Wes cupped the die in his hands. "All right," he said. "Anyway, it's even odds."

Was it?

## 88 THE SAME BUT NOT THE SAME

"I've got one cent more than a half-dollar," said Stan, checking the ten assorted coins in his hand.

"That's funny," Sally told him. "I've got exactly

the same, and in ten coins, but more pennies than
you."

What coins did each have?

## 89 ONLY THIS AND THAT

Add *this* to *that:*
        divide by three.
The square of *this,*
        you'll surely see.

But *that* to *this*
        is eight to one.
So figure what
        they are, for fun.

## 90 PAINTERS ON THE JOB

So they've painted the lamp posts on Main Street
at last. And this is the way it was.

Bill and Jake were to do the job, but Jake arrived early and started right away. He had just
finished three posts when Bill appeared on the scene.
"That's my side you've done," grumbled Bill.
"You're supposed to do the east side."

Jake laughed. "I'm easy," he said, carrying his
gear across the narrow street.

For a while they both painted. And then Bill
went over to Jake. "I've finished my side," he declared, "so I'll give you a hand."

"Okay," agreed Jake. "But we won't work on the
same post."

The job was soon completed. "You're a fine
painter," chuckled Jake. "The same number of posts
had to be done each side, but I've done twice as
many as you."

He was right. So how many had Bill painted?

## 91 THE JACKET

It's fun to wander around in Ben's little store. The old rascal has his own ideas on merchandising, and they do seem to pay off.

"What a revolting object," I commented, pointing to a cheap jacket aglitter with sequins. "Twenty-nine ninety-seven for that? Don't tell me you'll sell it!"

"Sure I will," said Ben. "At a fine profit too. At that price my percentage profit is exactly a third of the number of cents it cost me."

There's no accounting for tastes. But what had that jacket cost Ben?

## 92 TIME TO GO

"Well, it's time to go," said Jim, looking at his watch. "Ten o'clock, and you good people will need your sleep."

Tony laughed. "No hurry at all, and anyway tomorrow is Saturday." He also consulted his watch. "But I guess your ticker stopped a while ago. In two minutes' time it will be twice as many minutes short of eleven as it was past ten o'clock twenty-five minutes ago."

Most embarrassing! But what was the time?

## 93 BARGAIN PRICES

"Those sales!" Sally threw the parcel into a chair. "I got you some shirts at three dollars and the same number at one dollar, and now I wish I hadn't."

"You sure picked bargains," her husband declared. "Just what I need."

Sally sighed. "I know. But I'd have got four more for the same money if I'd spent half of it on each sort."

How many shirts had she bought?

## 94 A TOUGHIE! HOW MANY GIRLS?*

Those kids made a
        terrible noise!
Near to fifty in
        all with their toys,
The square of the square
Of the girls who were there
Came to double the
        cube of the boys.

## 95 FAIR IS FAIR

"I only want one, so three the same's no good to me," said Kim. "Anyway I've only got three dollars fifty."

Ron examined the little set of three identical stamps on the counter. "Okay. I'll pay the difference, and keep one for myself." He put down two one-dollar bills and two quarters. "They're quite a bargain, and we're sure to sell the other one."

So the boys bought the set for six dollars and left the store. Ron had been right, for they soon found a purchaser for the third stamp: even better, he paid them three dollars for it.

But then the trouble started! How were Kim and Ron to divide that three dollars fairly?

## 96 SENSE ABOUT CENTS

If Jack gave Jill one cent less than half of what Jill would have if Jill gave Jack one cent less than half of what Jack would have if Jack gave Jill one cent less than half of what Jill would have if Jill gave Jack one cent, he would then have just one cent more than Jill would have.

It seems a lot of fuss over very little, as they have only about fifty cents between the two of them. Can you figure out the exact amounts?

## 97 THE KNIGHT'S TOUR

| WAS | NOW | OLD | WAS | NOW |
|-----|-----|-----|------|------|
| AS | SUE | SAL | HALF | AS |
| IS | A | OLD | IS | WHEN |
| AS | SUE | SAL | THIRD | AS |

A complete sentence of twenty words is concealed here. If you start with the right word, and then follow the jumps of a chess knight from word to word along the correct route, a simple problem will be revealed.

A knight jumps two squares one way and one square at right angles—or *vice versa*—but only in the up-and-down and across directions.

Sue is in her teens, so how old is Sal?

## 98 ICY PATCHES

George took his brother's coat and cleared a chair for him by the fire. "How were the roads?" he asked. "They're bad around here."

"Even worse my way," John told him. "It took me just two hours dismal driving to get here. The last half of my route was on the highway, and there I averaged ten miles an hour better than the steady crawl I'd kept to for the first half. And the second hour I drove eight miles further than in the first."

Winter driving can be tough! How far had John driven?

## 99 THREE JOB LOTS*

"Did you buy anything?" asked Sarah, as her husband came into their store.

Sam nodded. "Two hundred and sixty dollars for three job lots I liked. We can always sell cheap shirts."

"If the quality's good, we can," agreed Sarah. "How many did you get then?"

Her husband searched his pockets. "I must have left my copy, but there were two hundred and sixty altogether," he replied. "In each lot they were priced at as many cents each as the number in that lot."

There would be an invoice with the shipment from the jobbers. But can you figure out the details of Sam's purchase?

## 100 THE SUMMER JOB

"Was that your bike, Dad?" asked Paul.

His father looked at the faded old photo. "My first, and I earned it," he replied. "I got a job that summer with a cycle dealer, and he was to pay me thirty bucks and this new bicycle for the seven weeks' work. But I quit after four weeks, so he gave me three dollars and I kept the bike."

What was its value?

## 101 RACING HOME

The three children trooped in, hot and excited. "We had a race," Jack told his mother. "All the way from Main."

"Who won?" she asked.

"Guess who," replied the boy. "Ann takes twenty-eight steps to run as far as Doug does in twenty-four steps or I do in twenty-one. But I take six steps while Doug takes seven and Ann eight."

Well! Who won?

## 102 SMALL-TOWN TALK

"That's a mix-up with the Drakes and the Todds," declared Amelia, set for a good old gossip. "You know the boys, Andy, Charles, and Bob Todd. They're in love with those Drake girls, Mary, Linda, and Nan."

Gwen never gossips, but she does know what goes on in the small community. "What mix-up?" she asked.

"Why, Andy's in love with Mary, but she dotes on Bob," replied her talkative neighbor. "And Bob wants Linda."

Gwen smiled, saying nothing. She knew none of those last statements could be true. All was well as between the three boys and the three girls, who were paired off happily, to their own and the parents' mutual satisfaction.

Incidentally, who loved whom in the three couples?

## 103 HAVE A CIGARETTE

"Cigarette?" asked Stan, offering an open pack. Les checked his own. "I've got more than you," he replied, "so you have one of mine."

Stan laughed. "Wrong brand, but I've never known you refuse before."

"Maybe I'm feeling generous today," his friend told him. "If you gave me a certain number from your pack, I'd have three times as many as you, but if I gave you that number instead, you'd have half as many as me."

How many cigarettes did Les have?

## 104 HIGH FINANCE

"Where's that little stone figure you bought last fall?" asked Mary, dusting Kim's room. "It was here on the dresser."

"Sold it to a kid at school, Mom," replied the boy. "For ninety-six cents."

"A funny amount," his mother commented. "Why not the even dollar?"

Kim grinned. "That's all he had, but I made as much per cent profit on the deal as what it cost me in cents."

What had the souvenir cost Kim?

## 105 TOO MUCH AND TOO LITTLE

Sam had been busy making his balance scales, and now the job was done. "Sit there," he told his sister, pointing to one of the rough slats he had as pans. "We'll see what you weigh."

"It won't be right," the girl protested, sitting there nevertheless. "It's not the same on each side."

The boy smiled, putting weights on the other crude pan. "I balanced it by shifting the center, and anyway we'll weigh you both sides and take the average."

So that's what he did, weighing her in each pan of his primitive contraption. One way she weighed a hundred pounds, but the other only sixty-four pounds.

What was her true weight?

## 106 A MATTER OF TASTE

Peter put down his fork. "I could use salt and pepper if I had them," he said.

The waitress shrugged. "Most folks don't ask for them," she told him.

"They don't come here then," Peter commented. "I've been watching. Some took only salt, some took pepper alone, some took both, and some took neither. Nine took salt, and eleven took pepper, and three times as many took both as those who took none."

How many customers had Peter observed?

## 107 FOOL'S GOLD

All was too quiet. There was no sound of splashing as John's father passed the bathroom.

Opening the door, he peeped in. And there was the boy, apparently conducting some sort of experiment in the filled wash basin.

"That's my paperweight," he exclaimed, spotting the gold-flecked hunk of ore lying there, immersed. "What's going on?"

John turned round, grinning. "I'm figuring out what happens," he explained. "I floated it in this little plastic bowl, and then I took it out and dropped it into the water. The bowl came up a bit, but does the water level in the basin rise or fall?"

A good question! What would you say?

## 108 HER LUCKY DAY

"Sorry I'm late," said Sally. "Been playing bridge at the Club, and I won just twenty-nine dollars."

"Wow!" exclaimed Doug. "That's something."

His wife grinned. "Three quick rubbers with Gwen, Judy, and Pat. We changed partners each rubber, and I was lucky"

Doug has his own views on her skill. "I'll say you were," he agreed tactfully.

"Well, we played one rubber at two dollars a hundred, one at three, and one at six. Payment to the nearest hundred points each time," explained Sally. "I won the first rubber with Judy, and she and Pat won the second. Pat won twenty-five dollars, and poor Gwen lost forty-nine."

That's how a man's money goes! What were the stakes for the final rubber?

## 109 A BALLAD OF BUTTON

A beery old boozer
        called Button
Ate ninety-four cents'
        worth of mutton.
Each cutlet cost seven,
Each chop cost eleven.
How much did he eat,
        that old glutton?

## 110 A FISHY STORY

"Did you catch anything?" asked Jane, turning from the sink as her husband strode into the kitchen. "I don't believe you men really go for the fishing!"

"Well, what about this?" chuckled Fred, sliding a fine trout on to a handy platter. "It weighs five-sevenths of its weight, and five-sevenths of a pound."

It was no great catch, but it did provide an alibi! What did Fred's fish weigh?

# SOLUTIONS TO PROBLEMS

## 1

Say $2X$ mammals went in but did not breed, and 600 other beasts went in but bred and increased to 9000. Then a total of $(X + 300)$ pairs went in, so a total of $23(X + 300)$ came out.

Hence $2X + 9000 = 23(X + 300)$; whence $X = 100$.

So 400 pairs—i.e., 800 beasts—went into the Ark.

## 2

Say he had driven $x$ miles, averaging $y$ miles per hour. Then, from his statements, we have:

$$\frac{x}{y+6} = \frac{x}{y} - \frac{5}{60} \quad \text{and} \quad \frac{x}{y-5} = \frac{x}{y} + \frac{6}{60},$$

So $72x = y(y + 6)$ and $50x = y(y - 5)$.

Hence $25y(y + 6) = 36y(y - 5)$, so $y = 30$.

Then $50x = 30 \times 25$, so $x = 15$.

He had driven 15 miles, averaging 30 miles per hour.

## 3

Say she had $\$X$ before her find. Then $(X + 2) = 5(X - 2)$, so $X = 3$.

Jill had $3.00 before her lucky find.

## 4

Represent the first digit of Joan's number by $X$, the last three digits by $Y$.

Then her number has the numerical value $(1000X + Y)$, and the transposed number the numerical value $(10Y + X)$.

So $10Y + X = \frac{3}{4}(1000X + Y) + 1$; whence $37Y - 2996X = 4$.

This has general solution $X = 37k + 4$, $Y = 2996k + 324$ (see Appendix C).

But $X$ is a single digit, so $k = 0$; hence $X = 4$ and $Y = 324$.

So Joan's number was 4324.

## 5

Say the regular envelopes cost $x\cancel{c}$. Then, depending on what was meant by "a quarter," we have $x + x + 25 = 72$, **OR** $x + 5x/4 = 72$.

The former gives $2x = 47$, with no whole-number solution. The latter gives $x = 32$.

So the air-mail envelopes cost 40$\cancel{c}$.

## 6

Say there were $x$ kids and $3x$ grown-ups, the total being $4x$. The total of all integers from 1 up to $4x$ is given by

$$\frac{4x(4x + 1)}{2} = 2x(4x + 1).$$

The grown-ups' numbers totaled three times the kid's numbers, so the total of all the numbers was a multiple of 4. Hence, from $2x(4x + 1)$, we see that $x$ must be even.

Since $2x(4x + 1) > 799$, $x > 8$.

Since $2x(4x + 1) < 1001$, $x < 12$.

So $x = 10$, making the total 820.

(*Note:* There were 10 kids and 30 grown-ups ahead.)

## 7

One of them had $x$ coffees @ 10¢, $y$ pieces of pie @ 15¢, and $z$ ice creams @ 20¢, where none of $x, y, z$ can be zero.

So $10x + 15y + 20z = 105$; hence $2x + 3y + 4z = 21$, which has possible solutions:

| | | | | | | | | |
|---|---|---|---|---|---|---|---|---|
| Coffees | $x$ .... | 1 | 1 | 2 | 3 | 4 | 5 | 7 |
| Pie | $y$ .... | 1 | 5 | 3 | 1 | 3 | 1 | 1 |
| Ices | $z$ .... | 4 | 1 | 2 | 3 | 1 | 2 | 1 |
| | | | | | | | | |
| Total items | .... | 6 | 7 | 7 | 7 | 8 | 8 | 9 |
| Total "eats" | .... | 5 | 6 | 5 | 4 | 4 | 3 | 2 |

Sam had as many coffees as the total of all items that each of the other two had. Hence, from the tabulation, Sam had 7 coffees, 1 pie, and 1 ice cream.

Then Ted and Joe each had 7 items, Ted's "eats" being more than Joe's. But they all had different numbers of ice creams, so we have: Ted, 2 coffees, 3 pies, and 2 ice creams; and Joe, 3 coffees, 1 pie, and 3 ice creams.

## 8

This type of problem has to be taken in great detail.

*Say Kibi was a boy.* In that case the second speaker must have been the mother, whose first statement must have been a lie and whose second statement must have been true. But Kalotan boys do not lie, so here we have a contradiction—which shows that Kibi was not a boy.

*Then Kibi was a girl.* If the first speaker was the father, then the second speaker was the mother whose first statement would be true and whose second statement would be a lie. In that case, Kibi would have spoken the truth and so would have said "I am a girl." But this implies that the first speaker, the father, lied, which must be impossible.

So the first speaker was the mother, and the second speaker was the father. Hence Kibi lied and so must have said "I am a boy." The first speaker, the mother, only made the one statement then, that being a lie.

Hence Kibi was a girl, the mother spoke first, and the father second.

### 9

Say $(x + 1)$ guests and Fanny had $y$ crackers. Then the rest of the guests ate $(3y - 1)$. So the over-all average per head was $(4y - 1)/(x + 1)$, the average without Fanny being $(3y - 1)/x$. Hence $(4y - 1)/(x + 1) - (3y - 1)/x = 1$; whence $x^2 - x(y - 1) + 3y - 1 = 0$. This is a quadratic equation in $x$.

Then $2x = (y - 1) \pm \sqrt{(y^2 - 14y + 5)}$.

Now $x$ and $y$ are whole numbers, so $(y^2 - 14y + 5)$ must be a perfect square.

Say, $y^2 - 14y + 5 = k^2$. This requires $y = 19$ and $k = 10$ (see Appendix D). So $x = 4$ or $14$.

But there were more than 6 guests; hence $x = 14$.

So there were 15 guests.

### 10

If the crab weighed $X$ pounds, $X = 3X/4 + 9/16$, so $X = 9/4$.

The crab weighed 2 lb. 4 oz.

### 11

Candle "A" burned one-sixth of its length per hour, candle "B" one-quarter of its length per hour. So, after $X$ hours,

"A" had burned $\dfrac{X}{6}$ of its length, leaving $\dfrac{6 - X}{6}$,

and

"B" had burned $\dfrac{X}{4}$ of its length, leaving $\dfrac{4-X}{4}$.

But, after $X$ hours, "A" was twice as long as "B," so

$$\dfrac{6-X}{6} = \dfrac{2(4-X)}{4} \; ; \text{ whence } X = 3.$$

The candles had burned for 3 hours.

## 12

If he ordered $N$ bushes, we have $N = 9a = 8b - 1 = 7c - 3$, where $a$, $b$, $c$ are unknown whole numbers.

Then $7c - 8b = 2$, with general solution $b = 7t - 2$ (see Appendix C).

Substituting this expression for $b$, we derive $56t - 9a = 17$, with general solution $t = 9k + 4$, $a = 56k + 23$.

$N = 9a$, so $N = 504k + 207$.

Now, $36N < 10000$, so $N < 278$. Hence $k = 0$ and $N = 207$.

Bill ordered 207 bushes.

## 13

Present ages: Ted, $X$; Clive $Y$; and Sue $(103 - X - Y)$.

Say Ted was twice as old as Sue, $k$ years ago. Then we have $X - k = 2(103 - X - Y - k)$; whence $k = 206 - X - 2Y$. At that time, Clive was $Y - k$, so $X + 3Y - 206 = 22$, which simplifies to $\qquad\qquad X + 3Y = 228$  (A)

Similarly, we derive $\qquad\qquad 3Y = 78$  (B)

Combining (A) and (B), $X = 50$ and $Y = 26$. Hence the three ages are: Ted, 50; Clive, 26; Sue, 27.

## 14

The clue to the solution of this is the fact that in the "magic square" with "magic constant" 15 the central cell contains 5: one third of 15.

Then, since $111 = 37 \times 3$, we can write 37 in the central cell of our semicompleted square. The remaining cells can then be filled in to give the required "magic constant" 111.

| 31 | 73 | 7  |
|----|----|----|
| 13 | 37 | 61 |
| 67 | 1  | 43 |

An interesting point about this "magic square" is that all nine numbers are prime numbers.

## 15

The cup alone was $1.25, the saucer 25¢.

## 16

Say that special last day of a month was $N$, with $(N - 1)$ previous days in that month.

In any year there are 7 long months and 5 short months.

If it was a short month, $(N - 1) + (7 - 4) = 31$; whence $N = 29$. In that case, the date was February 29. But $29 = 18 + 11$ or $19 + 10$, implying the year 1811 or 1910. Neither of these could be a "leap year," so it could not have been a short month.

It was a long month, with $N = 31$ and $(N - 1)$ $= 30$.

Then, $30 + (6 - 5) = 31$, so there were also 31 days in the following month: hence the month must have been July, this and August being the only two successive months of 31 days.

$31 = 18 + 13$ or $19 + 12$, implying the year 1813 or 1912.

Since Sam "turned up the radio," he could not have met Susan in the year 1813! Hence that special date was July 31, 1912.

## 17

Say: $x$ @ 59¢, $y$ @ $1.04, $z$ @ 83¢, $(12 - x - y - z)$ @ $1.39.

Then $80x + 35y + 56z = 468$, $x$, $y$, and $z$ being whole numbers.

Dividing by 7 (see Appendix C), we get: $x = 7k + 2$.

So $x = 9$ or 2.

If $x = 9$, we would have $35y + 56z = -252$, a negative number.

Hence $x = 2$, so $5y + 8z = 44$; whence $y = 4$ and $z = 3$.

He ordered 2 @ 59¢, 4 @ $1.04, 3 @ 83¢, and 3 @ $1.39.

## 18

This is a really tricky one! But the solution is not difficult.

"Half of what I'd be" must be a whole number, so "what I'd be" must be an even number. Hence "what I am" cannot end with 1.

We tabulate the four possible arrangements of the three digits, the one unknown digit being taken as $A$.

What I am ...... 1 *A* 3   1 3 *A*   3 1 *A*   *A* 1 3
What I'd be .... 3 *A* 4   3 4 *A*   4 3 *A*   *A* 3 4

"What I am" is "nine less than half what I'd be," so the last three pairs of arrangements listed above cannot be acceptable. Hence "what I am" must be 1 *A* 3, with "value" $(10A + 103)$.

Then, from the data given, $10A + 103 = (10A + 304)/2 - 9$; whence $A = 8$. So I am 183.

## 19

Jim gave up 1 apple, so received 3¢. Paul gave up 3 apples, so received 9¢.

## 20

There are only two different selections of 12 coins to total 49¢: either 4 pennies, 7 nickels, and 1 dime or 9 pennies, 1 nickel, 1 dime, and 1 quarter.

So Peter had the 1 quarter, and the coins each had were as detailed above.

## 21

Say Aunt Annie was $x$ years old. Therefore $x = 5(x + 5) - 5(x - 5)$; whence $x = 50$. So she was 50 years old.

## 22

Including the bonus snowdrops, the lots that were ordered would entail: re daffodils, 22 bulbs for $1.98; re tulips, 37 for $1.48 and 37 for $1.98.

Say he ordered $x$ lots of daffodils, $y$ lots of tulips

@ \$1.48, and $z$ lots of tulips @ \$1.98.

Then, re cost, $198x + 148y + 198z = 4000$;

whence                 $99x + 74y + 99z = 2000$ (A),

re bulbs, $22x + 37y + 37z = 880$;

whence                 $44x + 74y + 74z = 1760$ (B).

Subtracting (B) from (A) we have:

$$55x + 25z = 240;$$

whence                 $11x + 5z = 48,$

so $x = 3, z = 3$.

Substituting for $x$ and $z$, in (A) or (B), we have $y = 19$.

Hence Bob ordered 3 lots of daffs, 19 lots of tulips @ \$1.48, and 3 lots of tulips @ \$1.98.

## 23

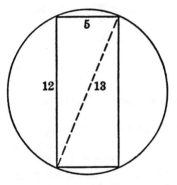

Every picture tells a story, and Pythagoras gave us the clue here: $13^2 = 5^2 + 12^2$.

The *hole* would be 12 inches deep.

## 24

A diagram will be self-explanatory, noting that they were at "A" when Jeff complained first and at "B" when he stopped.

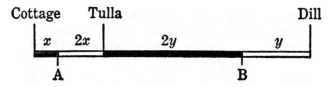

Clearly, $2x + 2y = 8$, so $3x + 3y = 12$. Hence the distance from the cottage to Dill was 12 miles.

## 25

Taking amounts in cents, the present rate is $X$. In 4 hours he earns $4X$. For twice that, in 7 hours, the rate would be $8X/7$. At that rate, in 5 hours he would earn $40X/7$. For 1¢ more than that, in 3 hours, the rate would be $(40X + 7)/21$.

So $(40X + 7)/21 = X + 70$; whence $X = 77$. The present rate is 77¢ per hour.

## 26

Re left-hand pocket, 1 dime and 1 quarter total 35¢.

Re right-hand pocket, 5 dimes = 2 quarters.

Say he had $2X$ cents worth of coins in each pocket.

Then in left-hand pocket he had $2X/35$ dimes, $2X/35$ quarters; in right-hand pocket he had $X/10$ dimes, $X/25$ quarters.

Then ratio of dimes to quarters was $(2/35 + 1/10)$ to $(2/35 + 1/25)$; i.e., 55 to 34.

He had whole numbers of each, so say $55k$ dimes and $34k$ quarters, where $k$ is some whole number. The total value, then, would be $1400k$ cents. But he had less than $20, so $k = 1$, making the total $14.00.

(*Note:* Although this was not asked for, it can be ascertained that he had: in left-hand pocket, 20 dimes, 20 quarters; in right-hand pocket, 35 dimes, 14 quarters.)

## 27

One solution would be as follows. Fill 11-oz. measure and then fill 5-oz. measure from it. Empty 5-oz. measure into the bottle, and fill it again from 11-oz. measure. Empty 5-oz. measure into the bottle, and then pour the remaining 1 oz. into it from the 11-oz. measure. Finally, fill the 11-oz. measure from the bottle, so leaving 12 oz. in the bottle.

## 28

Total weight was $X$ lb., $Y$ oz., so Sam took $4(16X + Y)¢$. Hence $64X + 4Y = 100X + Y$, whence $Y = 12X$. But $Y < 16$, so $X = 1$, $Y = 12$.

Sam had sold 1 lb. 12 oz. of jelly beans for total of $1.12.

## 29

We have $40 = 1 \times 2 \times 2 \times 2 \times 5$, so the possible ages of the three children must have been one of the following trios:

|  | 20 | 10 | 10 | 8 | 5 |
|---|---|---|---|---|---|
|  | 2 | 4 | 2 | 5 | 4 |
|  | 1 | 1 | 2 | 1 | 2 |
| Totals | 23 | 15 | 14 | 14 | 11 |

Bill must have known the house number. But he still could not be sure of the ages. So the house number must have been 14.

When told that the two eldest were walking home from school, he realized that the ages must be 8, 5, and 1 years.

### 30

Say Ted had dealt himself $x$ cards. Then consider each of the possible situations as regards the four players:

I.        $x$            Dropped: $2x - 1$. Dealt: $4x$
  (Ted) $x$       $x$      Undealt:  $53 - 6x$, which
         $x$                        cannot be a multiple of 3.

II.      $x + 1$        Dropped: $2x - 1$, **OR** $2x$.
  (Ted) $x$     $x$        Dealt: $4x$
         $x$            If $2x - 1$ dropped, Undealt
                         $= 52 - 6x$, not a multiple
                         of 3.
                       If $2x$ dropped, Undealt $= 51$
                         $- 6x$, so Bob had $17 - 2x$.
                         $17 - 2x = x$ **OR** $x + 1$,
                         with no integral solution.

III.     $x + 1$        Dropped: $2x$. Dealt: $4x + 2$.
  (Ted) $x$      $x + 1$  Undealt:  $50 - 6x$, which
         $x$                        cannot be a multiple
                                    of 3.

IV.      $x + 1$        Dropped: $2x$, **OR** $2x + 1$.
  (Ted) $x$      $x + 1$  Dealt: $4x + 3$.
         $x + 1$        If $2x$ dropped, Undealt $= 49$
                         $- 6x$, not a multiple of 3.
                       If $2x + 1$ dropped, Undealt
                         $= 48 - 6x$, so Bob had
                         $16 - 2x$. $16 - 2x = x +$
                         $1$, whence $x = 5$. 11 cards
                         dropped.

Hence 11 cards had been dropped, and at that moment Ted had dealt himself 5 cards, with 6 cards to each of the others.

### 31

If there were $2x$ cigars originally, then Ted left $x$. He had smoked $x$ cigars. So $x^2/9 = x$; whence $x = 9$.
His father had had 18 cigars.

## 32

Divide the complete circle into 60 units, the 12 o'clock mark corresponding to zero (or 60). Then in those units at $Y$ minutes after $X$ hours, the hands will be at positions:

hour hand, $5X + \dfrac{Y}{12}$; minute hand, $Y$.

Here we have $Y = 5X + \dfrac{Y}{12} + 1$, so $11Y - 60X = 12$. Since $Y < 60$, the required solution is $X = 2$, $Y = 12$. (Appendix C).

Ann returned at 2.12 a.m.

## 33

Stamps: $a$ @ 1¢, $b$ @ 2¢, $c$ @ 3¢, $d$ @ 5¢, $(17 - a - b - c - d)$ @ 10¢. Then $a + 2b + 3c + 5d + 10(17 - a - b - c - d) = 10k$, where $k$ is some whole number. Dividing through by 5, $(a + 2b + 3c)$ must be a multiple of 5, since all are whole numbers. But we are restricted to two 4's and three 3's for $a$, $b$, $c$, etc. If $b = c$, then we have $a$ as a multiple of 5, which is impossible. So $b = 3$, $c = 4$, or vice versa. Quick trial of these two possibilities shows that $(a + 2b + 3c)$ is divisible by 5 only with $b = 4$, $c = 3$, $a = 3$.

Substituting these values in the original equation, and simplifying, we have $d = 2(9 - k)$. Hence $d$ must be even, so $d = 4$.

She bought: 3 @ 1¢, 4 @ 2¢, 3 @ 3¢, 4 @ 5¢, 3 @ 10¢.

## 34

Say the digits of her age were $X$ and $Y$ in that order, with numerical value $(10X + Y)$.

The "reverse" would be seen as $Y$ and $X$, in that

order, with numerical value $(10Y + X)$.

So $\dfrac{10Y + X}{3} + 34 = 10X + Y$;

whence $29X - 7Y = 102$.

This has general solution $X = 7k - 3$ (see Appendix C).

But $X$ is a digit, so $k = 1$, with $X = 4$ and $Y = 2$.

Her age was 42 years.

### 35

Say, he drove $Y$ miles at $X$ m.p.h.

$(Y - 20)$ miles at $\dfrac{2X}{3}$ m.p.h. would take $\dfrac{3Y - 60}{2X}$

hours, and 20 minutes less than that is $\dfrac{9Y - 180 - 2X}{6X}$ hours.

In that time, at $X$ m.p.h., he would drive $\dfrac{9Y - 180 - 2X}{6}$ miles.

So $\dfrac{9Y - 180 - 2X}{6} = Y - 10$;

whence $3Y - 2X = 120$.    (A)

Similarly, re the second paragraph, we have $Y + X = 100$  (B)

Combining (A) and (B) (see Appendix A), $X = 36$ and $Y = 64$.

Sam drove 64 miles.

### 36

Take ages as Tom, $X$ years and Ted, $Y$ years. Then $X - 7 = 3(Y - 7)$, and $X + 7 = 2(Y + 7)$. So $X = 49$ and $Y = 21$.

Tom was 49 years old.

## 37

Say he worked $X$ days the previous month.
Then $14X = 28.9$, or $29.9$, or $30.9$, or $31.9$.
But $X$ is a whole number, so $14X = 28.9$;
whence $X = 18$.
Bill worked 18 days.

## 38

The lots totaled 89 buttons (i.e., 5, 6, 12, 14, 23, 29), and when one lot was taken, there must have remained a multiple of 3. So there are four basic possibilities, which can be tabulated:

| She took | 5 or | 14 or | 23 or | 29 |
|---|---|---|---|---|
| Leaving | 84 | 75 | 66 | 60 |
| Which would be: red | 56 | 50 | 44 | 40 |
| blue | 28 | 25 | 22 | 20 |
| Remaining lots | 6 | 5 | 5 | 5 |
| | 12 | 6 | 6 | 6 |
| | 14 | 12 | 12 | 12 |
| | 23 | 23 | 14 | 14 |
| | 29 | 29 | 29 | 23 |
| Blue lots | — | — | — | 6, 14 |
| Red lots | — | — | — | 5, 12, 23 |

Only with the numbers shown in the fourth column would it be possible to have the requisite totals of red and blue.
So 29 buttons were taken.

## 39

Say the digits of the total were $X$ and $Y$ in that order. Then we have $10X + Y = 2XY - 7$; whence $(2X - 1)(Y - 5) = 12$.
Since $X$ and $Y$ are digits, $(2X - 1)$ and $(Y - 5)$

must both be whole numbers: also $(2X - 1)$ must be odd, and $(Y - 5) < 5$.

So $(2X - 1) = 3$, $(Y - 5) = 4$; whence $X = 2$ and $Y = 9$.

There were 29 persons at the dinner.

### 40

Say Sam walked $x$ m.p.h. When he started, Dad was 1½ miles ahead; and 1 hour later, being overtaken at $(x - 3)$ m.p.h., he was $(9 - 2x)/2$ miles ahead. But, by Hank's statement, Dad was ¼ mile ahead. Hence $x = 4¼$.

When Sam left Hank, 35 minutes later, Dad was 2 miles ahead.

Since Sam overtook at 1¼ m.p.h., he would catch Dad in 1 hr. 36 mins.

Altogether, then, Sam would have walked for 2 hr. 36 mins., so the total distance was 221/20; i.e., $11\frac{1}{20}$ miles.

### 41

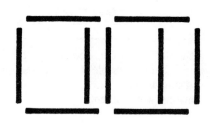

### 42

Say length of head was $2X$ feet. Then $6X + 3X = 27/2$, so $2X = 3$.

The head was 3 feet long.

## 43

Since 10 is not divisible by 3, the number of dimes Jack had when Jill spoke must have been a multiple of 3. Say he had $3X$ dimes when Jill spoke; i.e., $30X\phi$. Then half of what he had spent was equal to $20X\phi$. So he had spent $40X\phi$.

Hence that morning he must have had $70X\phi$ altogether. But that amount was "almost a dollar," so $X = 1$, and he had spent $40\phi$.

## 44

Say the kennel cost $X$, and the dog $Y$.

Then $Y = \dfrac{X + 5 + Y}{3}$, and $X = \dfrac{3(X + Y - 5)}{4}$.

Then $2X - Y = 5$, and $3X - Y = 15$; whence $X = 10$, $Y = 15$.

So the dog cost $15.00.

## 45

This can be solved simply by setting up a tabulation, bearing in mind that only one child spoke the truth.

| Guilty | Truth spoken by |
|--------|-----------------|
| John   | Ann and Sally   |
| Gail   | John and Sally  |
| Ann    | Sally and Gail  |
| Sally  | Gail alone      |

So Sally was the culprit.

## 46

Say there were $x$ dimes, $y$ nickels, and $(70 - x - y)$ pennies.

Then $10x + 5y + (70 - x - y) = 117$, so $9x + 4y = 47$. This has general solution (see Appendix C) $x = 4k - 1$, $y = 14 - 9k$. Here we must have $k = 1$, so $x = 3$ and $y = 5$.

Uncle Ken had 3 dimes, 5 nickels, and 62 pennies.

### 47

Say each bought $X$ pears. Then $10X/3 - 25X/8$ 5, so $X = 24$.

They each bought 24 pears.

### 48

Say "this" is $x$. Then, $3(1 + \frac{1}{2}x) + 4 = x +$ 23, so $x = 32$.

Hence "this" is 32.

### 49

Charlie was Tom's grandson.

### 50

Say Steve wanted frame $X$ inches by $Y$ inches. From his statements we have $6 + 2X/3 = 20$, and $6 + 15 = Y$, so $X = 21$ and $Y = 21$.

He wanted the frame to be 21 by 21 inches.

### 51

Say the smallest of the four tables had $x$ tiles to the side, and the "old relic" had $y$ tiles to the side.

Then $x^2 + (x + 6)^2 + (x + 12)^2 + (x + 18)^2 = y^2$, so $4x^2 + 72x + 504 = y^2$, whence $(2x + 18)^2 + 180 = y^2$ (see Appendix D).

Then $y^2 - (2x + 18)^2 = 180 = 2^2 \times 3^2 \times 5$.
So we must have $y + (2x + 18) = 18$ or $30$ or $90$
with $y - (2x + 18) = 10 \qquad 6 \qquad 2$

| subtracting | $4x + 36 =$ | 8 | 24 | 88 |
| whence | $x =$ | — | — | 13 |
| with | $y =$ | — | — | 46 |

Altogether then, there were $46^2$ tiles; i.e., 2116 tiles.

### 52

Say $x$ men and $y$ women; then *kaazi* $= 2z$, since "half *kaazi*" must be a whole number.

If a third of the men had been women and half the women men, there would have been $y/2 + x/3 = (2x + 3y)/6$ women. So $y = \dfrac{2x + 3y}{6} + 11$; whence $3y - 2x = 66$.

If $2z$ women had been men, and $z$ women had not been there at all, there would have been $(y - 3z)$ women. So $x = 2(y - 3z)$   (A).

Hence $2x = 3y - 66$, and $2x = 4y - 12z$, so $y = 12z - 66$.

Substituting for $y$ in equation (A), we have $x = 18z - 132$.

Now $y > x$, so $18z - 132 < 12z - 66$; hence $z < 11$.

Also, $x + y > 100$, so $30z - 198 > 100$; hence $z > 9$.

So we must have $z = 10$; whence $x = 48$, $y = 54$.

*Kaazi* is Kalotan for twenty, and there were 48 men at the party.

### 53

This is a matter of numerical notation. We normally use the decimal notation (i.e., base 10) when writing. When we write 34, we mean "three tens, plus four units" : our 217 means "two hundreds, plus one ten, plus seven units."

Say they use a notation based on $X$ in Kalota (i.e., base $X$). Then, $4X + 4$ is the number that we call forty: hence $X$ is the number that we call nine. This is confirmed by the fact that $3X + 3$ must be the number we call thirty, which is "six times five."

Now "four times five times seven" is the number that we call "one hundred and forty." This can be broken down as "one times nine squared, plus six nines, plus five units" and would therefore be written as 165 in the Kalotan base-9 notation.

(*Note:* Decimal notation words, such as "forty" and "hundred," have no meaning in connection with notations of other bases. Hence in this case we must not say "forty-four," "thirty-three," etc. In words we would describe the number 165 merely as "one six five.")

### 54

Say $X$ knives and $Y$ forks. Then, $49X + 39Y = 527$, the general solution for which is $X = 39k + 2$, $Y = 11 - 49k$ (see Appendix C).

Obviously, $k = 0$ here. So $X = 2$ and $Y = 11$. Mike bought 2 knives and 11 forks.

### 55

Say the ages were Jack $X$ and Jill $Y$ years.

Working back, from Jack's words:

when Jack was 2 years younger, Jill was $(Y - 2)$;

when Jack was $(Y - 2)$, Jill was $(2Y - X - 2)$ (A).

in 2 years time, Jack would be $(X + 2)$;

one-third of that is $(X + 2)/3$ (B).

Combining (A) and (B), $4X - 6Y = -8$, so $2X - 3Y = -4$ (C).

Working back, from Jill's words:

when Jack was "twice as old as Jill was," the ages

were Jack $(2X - 2Y)$, Jill $(X - Y)$;

when Jill was $(2X - 2Y + 3)$, Jack was $(3X - 3Y + 3)$;

when Jill is $(3X - 3Y + 3)$, Jack will be $(4X - 4Y - 3)$;

hence, $4X - 4Y - 3 = X + 1$, so $3X - 4Y = -2$  (D).

Combining (C) and (D), we derive $X = 10$, $Y = 8$ (see Appendix A).

So the ages were Jack 10 and Jill 8 years.

### 56

The only times that the hands are right angles at an exact minute are at 3:00 o'clock and 9:00 o'clock. Hence Jack must have been referring to 3:00 p.m. when he said "last time the two hands were at right angles this afternoon."

At 3:00 p.m., it was 30 minutes before "the half-hour."

"At the next minute," then, it would be 60 seconds (i.e., twice 30) after the same "half-hour." Hence it would be 3:31 p.m.

### 57

Say he had: in left hand; $x$ pennies, $a$ ¢ in other coins;

in right hand; $y$ nickels, $b$ ¢ in other coins.

Their total value would be: $x + 5y + a + b$ cents.

From his 1st statement:

$10x + a + y + b = x + 5y + a + b + 100$

so        $9x - 4y = 100$   (A).

From his 2nd statement:

$5x + a + 10y + b = 2x + 10y + 2a + 2b$

so              $3x = a + b$   (B).

From (A) and (B), we have $4(y + 25) = 3(a + b)$  (C).

Now from (B), we see that $(a + b)$ must be multiple of 3, and from (C), we see that $(a + b)$ must be multiple of 4. So $(a + b)$ must be multiple of 12—say $a + b = 12k$, where $k$ is some whole number.

Then, from (B), we have $x = 4k$; and from (C), $y = 9k - 25$.

From his final statement, a minimum solution is required. But, since $y$ cannot be negative, $k > 2$, so we have $k = 3$; whence $x = 12$, $y = 2$. Then $a + b = 36$. The minimum number of coins to make up 36¢ is three; i.e., 1 penny, 1 dime, 1 quarter.

So he had altogether: 13 pennies, 2 nickels, 1 dime, and 1 quarter.

## 58

It's impossible to do it! Each domino must cover one white and one black square on the checkerboard. Two white or two black squares have been removed. So, irrespective of the placing of the dominoes, there must be two black or two white squares left uncovered.

## 59

Say he bought $x$ pairs @ 50¢, $y$ pairs @ $1.50, and $(12 - x - y)$ pairs @ $2.

Then totaling the costs, $y + 3x = 24$, so $y = 24 - 3x$.

Hence $x + y = 24 - 2x$, which must be less than 12: so $x > 6$.

Also, since $y = 24 - 3x$, we must have $x < 8$.

So $x = 7$, with $y = 3$.

He bought 7 pairs @ 50¢, 3 pairs @ $1.50, and 2 pairs @ $2.

## 60

Say she bought: $a$ @ 10¢, $b$ @ 15¢, $c$ @ 25¢, and $d$ @ 40¢.

Then $10a + 15b + 25c + 40d = 100k$, where $k$ is some whole number.

So $2a + 3b + 5c + 8d = 20k$.

It is clear that $b$ and $c$ must both be even or both odd.

If they are both even, then $b = c = 10$, and $a = d = 5$. This gives $20k = 130$, entailing $k = 13/2$, which is not a whole number.

So they are both odd, and $b = c = 5$, with $a = d = 10$. This gives $20k = 140$, so $k = 7$.

Hence she bought 5 each @ 15¢ and 25¢ and 10 each @ 10¢ and 40¢, at a total cost of $7.00.

## 61

When they wed say his age was $x$ years, and hers $(x - 6)$ years.

Then 9 years later their ages would be $(x + 9)$ and $(x + 3)$.

So $(x + 9)/(x + 3) = 14/12$; whence $x = 33$.

He was 33 years old, and she was 27 when they wed.

## 62

Say the true time was $x$ hours and $y$ minutes, both $x$ and $y$ being whole numbers with $y < 60$.

Steve's watch had gained $\dfrac{60x + y}{60}$ minutes, so showed $\dfrac{60x + 61y}{60}$ minutes after the hour.

1 hour earlier, Doug's watch had lost

$$\frac{2\,[60(x-1)+y]}{60}\text{ minutes, so showed }\frac{58y-120x+120}{60}$$

minutes after the hour.

$$\text{So }\frac{60x+61y}{60}=\frac{2(58y-120x+120)}{60};\text{ whence}$$

$60x - 11y = 48$.

This has general solution $x = 11k + 3$, $y = 60k + 12$ (see Appendix C). But $y < 60$; hence $k = 0$, and $x = 3$, $y = 12$.

The true time was 3:12 p.m.

## 63

Say there were: 6 students under 11, $x$ between 11 and 12, $x$ between 12 and 13, and $y$ aged 13 years and over. The total was $(2x + y + 6)$.

Then $2x + 6 = y$, and $x + 6 = (2x + y + 6)/3$. Hence $x = 6$, $y = 18$ (see Appendix A).

There were 36 students in the class.

## 64

Say Sally will be $x$ years old tomorrow. When her boy friend was 3 years older than half of $(x - 1)$, he was $(x + 5)/2$.

If she were 4 years younger than three times that, she'd be $(3x + 7)/2$.

1 year younger than half that would be $(3x + 3)/4$.

Now if she were 10 years younger, tomorrow she'd be $(x - 10)$.

So $x - 10 = (3x + 3)/4$; whence $x = 43$.

Sally will be 43 years old tomorrow.

## 65

Say the border would be $x$ feet wide. Then $(8 - 2x) (15 - 2x) = 60$; whence $x = 1\frac{1}{2}$.

The border must be 18 inches wide, but neither 4-inch nor 5-inch tiles can provide this.

So 3-inch tiles were needed.

## 66

The "completed years of service," 2, 5, 6, 7 totaled 20 years.

Say the men (or man) had 3 points per year for total $x$ years, and girls (or girl) had 2 points per year for total $(20 - x)$ years.

Then the grand total points was $(3x + 40 - 2x)$; i.e., $(x + 40)$ points, which must be a factor of 23000.

Then $k(x + 40) = 23000$, where $k$ is some whole number.

There was at least one girl, with at least 2 years service, so $x$ cannot exceed 18. Hence $k$ cannot be less than 23000/58, so $k > 396$.

There was at least one man, with at least 2 years service, so $(x + 40)$ cannot be less than 42; whence $k < 548$.

The factors of 23000 are $2^3 \times 5^3 \times 23$.

There are only two pairs of factors for 23000, with one factor (i.e., $k$) lying in the range 397 to 547. These form the basis for the following tabulation:

$$k = 460 \text{ or } 500$$
$$(x + 40) = 50 \qquad 46$$
$$\text{whence } x = 10 \qquad 6$$

But no combination of 2, 5, 6, 7 can total 10. Hence $x = 6$, with $k = 500$, from which we see that each point was worth $5.

Since $x = 6$, there was only one man and he had 6 years service: the other three must have been girls with 2, 5, and 7 years service.

The $230 was shared as: 1 man, $90; 3 girls, $70, $50, $20.

## 67

Say their ages "now" were: Paul, $3X$; Hettie, $2X$ years. Then 4 years ago their ages were $(3X - 4)$ and $(2X - 4)$ years.

So $3X - 4 = 2(2X - 4)$; whence $X = 4$.

Hence Paul was 12 and Hettie 8 years old.

## 68

A solution is $123 + 4 - 5 + 67 - 89 = 100$.

## 69

Say their ages are Gwen, $x$; Dean, $y$; and Bill, $z$ years.

$a$ years hence, when Gwen will be twice as old as Dean (will be), their ages will be Gwen, $x + a$, and Dean, $y + a$.

So $x + a = 2y + 2a$; whence $a = x - 2y$. At that time, then, Bill will be $z + x - 2y$; hence $x - 2y + z = 17$   (A).

$b$ years ago, when Dean was twice as old as Bill (was), their ages were Dean, $y - b$, and Bill, $z - b$.

So $y - b = 2z - 2b$; whence $b = 2z - y$. At that time, then, Gwen was $x - (2z - y)$; hence $x + y - 2z = 23$   (B).

Taking equations (A) and (B), $x + y - 2z = 23$, and $x - 2y + z = 17$; whence $y - z = 2$. So Bill is 2 years younger than Dean.

When Dean was 10, Bill must have been 8 years old.

## 70

Ted held out more than 3 days, so Sam held out more than 5 days. Hence from that Monday to that Tuesday was at least 8 days, so Sam held out at least 8 days longer than Ted.

But Sam held out "half as long again" as Ted, so Ted must have held out at least 16 days.

Assuming that Ted held out 16 days, then Sam held out 24 days, and Joe 32 days. This solution complies with all conditions.

If Ted held out more than 16 days, then the "Monday to Tuesday" requirement would imply that Sam held out 15 days longer than Ted, which would entail Sam having held out for more than one month. So this is unacceptable.

Hence Joe held out for 32 days.

## 71

From the statements made, the rocks were equidistant from Dill, Penn Point, and Jim's dock. So the rocks would lie at the center of a circle passing through those three points, the line joining Penn Point and Dill being a diameter. Hence the triangle joining the three points was a right-angled triangle.

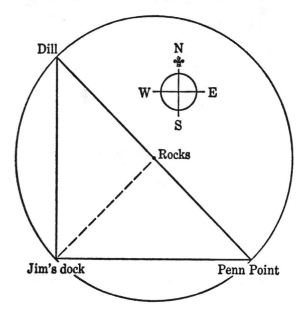

Since Dill was due north from Jim's dock, the course to Penn Point would be due east.

## 72

Say he started with $x$ ¢, and entered $n$ booths.

Then at the 1st he paid $10 + (x - 10)/2 - 1$; i.e., $(x + 8)/2$ ¢.

He left the successive booths with:

1st $\dfrac{(x - 8)}{2}$ ¢, 2nd $\dfrac{(x - 24)}{4}$ ¢, 3rd $\dfrac{(x - 56)}{8}$ ¢,

etc.

The *pattern* is clear, and we see that he must have left the $n$th booth with $\dfrac{x - 8(2^n - 1)}{2^n} = 7$¢.

Hence $x + 8 = 15 \times 2^n$

Now obviously we have $n > 1$, so $(x + 8)$ is a multiple of 60.

Hence, say $x = 60k - 8$, where $k$ is some power of 2.

But $x > 500$, so $k > 8$ (i.e., $2^3$).

Also, $x < 1007$, so $k < 17$.

Hence $k = 16$, with $x = 952$, and $n = 6$.

He started with $9.52 and entered 6 booths.

## 73

Say Larry had $X$ guinea pigs and $Y$ parakeets. Then $4X + 2Y = 50$, and $X + Y = 15$. Thence, $X = 10$ and $Y = 5$ (see Appendix A).

So Larry had 10 guinea pigs.

## 74

Say she bought $x$ yards @ $x$ ¢, and $y$ yards @ $y$ ¢.

Then $x^2 - y^2 = 215$, and $x^2 + y^2 < 1000$

Now $x^2 - y^2 = (x + y)(x - y)$, and $215 =$ $215 \times 1$ or $43 \times 5$

so $\qquad x + y = 215$ or $43$
with $\qquad x - y = \quad 1$ or $\quad 5$

hence $\qquad 2x \qquad = 216$ or $48$
and $\qquad\qquad 2y = 214$ or $38$
so $\qquad\quad x \qquad = 108$ or $24$
and $\qquad\qquad y = 107$ or $19$

But $x^2 + y^2 < 1000$; hence $x = 24$ and $y = 19$.

Ann bought 24 yards of one material and 19 yards of the other.

## 75

Say the first digit of her age is $X$. Then her age can be expressed in years as $10X + 3$: its reverse as $30 + X$.

Then $X^2 = 30 + X$; whence $X = 6$.

Her age was 63 years.

## 76

Say the rent was $\$x$. It could be paid 1 way in $1 bills, 3 ways using $(x - 1)$ $1 bills, 5 ways using $(x - 2)$ $1 bills, and so on, until we come to $(2x + 1)$ ways using no $1 bills.

So the total number of ways is $1 + 3 + 5 + 7 +$ ........ $+ (2x + 1)$, which equals $(x + 1)^2$.

8 years is 416 weeks, 9 years is 468 weeks, and $441 = 21^2$.

So $x + 1 = 21$; hence $x = 20$.

The rent was $20 weekly.

## 77

Jack had $x$ ¢ and Jill $y$ ¢. So $x = 75 + \frac{3}{4}y$, and $y = 50 + \frac{1}{2}x$. Hence, $4x - 3y = 300$, and $x -$

$2y = -100$; whence $x = 180$ and $y = 140$. (See Appendix A). Jack had \$1.80, and Jill \$1.40.

## 78

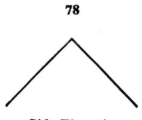

*Side Elevation*

This could be a wire figure, in the form of an ellipse, *folded* at its smaller "diameter."

## 79

Pete figured on $x$ days including $y$ Saturdays. So we have $10x + 20y = 12x$; whence $x = 10y$. He referred to "Saturdays," however, so $y > 1$. If $y = 3$, then $x = 30$, but there must be at least 4 Saturdays in 30 days, so this is impossible. Hence $y = 2$, with $x = 20$.

Pete's mother gave him \$2.40.

## 80

Say there were $(x + y + z + w)$ questions, and Ann and Bill both answered the same $x$ questions rightly. Then we can tabulate their respective performances as follows:

|      | Right   | Wrong   |
|------|---------|---------|
| Ann  | $x + y$ | $z + w$ |
| Bill | $x + z$ | $y + w$ |

From the statements made:

$x + y = 2z + 2w, y + w = 5, x + y + z =$ ¾ $(x + y + z + w)$; whence $3x + 11y = 40$ (see Appendix C).

Both $x$ and $y$ are whole numbers, and not negative, so $x = 6$ and $y = 2$. Then $w = 3$, with $z = 1$.

There were 12 questions. Ann answered 8 correctly.

## 81

From Jack's reply to the second question, whatever cash he had must have been a multiple of 4 in cents. So, say he had $4X$¢. Then, depending on what he meant by "a quarter," we have two different equations:

$4X + 25 + 100 = 6X$ **OR** $5X + 100 = 6X$;
i.e., $2X = 125$ **OR** $X = 100$.

Since 125 is not a multiple of 2, the second alternative must have applied. Then $4X = 400$.

Jack had $4.00.

## 82

If a triangle with sides $a, b, c$ is inscribed in a circle of radius $r$, then:

$$r = \frac{abc}{4\sqrt{s(s-a)(s-b)(s-c)}}, \text{ where } 2s = a + b + c.$$

So here we have $r = \dfrac{25 \times 13}{16}$.

Circumference $= 2\pi r = \dfrac{2 \times 22 \times 25 \times 13}{7 \times 16}$ approximately; i.e., 127½ feet.

For "comfortable fit," 127 tiles would just do the job.

## 83

Say check was for $X and $Y$ cents, then Simon received $Y and $X$ cents.

So $(X + 100Y) - 35 = 2(100X + Y)$; whence $98Y - 199X = 35$. This has general solution $X = 98k + 21$, $Y = 199k + 43$ (see Appendix C).

$Y < 100$, so $k = 0$; hence $X = 21$ and $Y = 43$. The check was for $21.43.

## 84

Say the hourly rate is $X$¢, and "work back" from the comma.

In 40 hours Peter earns $40X$¢. If Pam earned that amount weekly, in 4 weeks she would earn $160X$¢; i.e., $8X/5$ dollars.

If Peter earned that number of cents an hour, his hourly rate would be $8X/5$¢. So $8X/5 = X + 87$; whence $X = 145$.

So Peter's hourly rate is $1.45.

## 85

Alan painted $a$ per hour and Ben $b$ per hour. That day, in $k$ hours, they had painted $k(a + b)$, so $10a + b = k(a + b)$. The following day they would paint $(k + 1)(a + b) = 10b + a$. So, $k(a + b) = 10a + b = 10b + a - a - b$; whence $5a = 4b$. But $a$ and $b$ must be whole numbers, each less than 10, so $a = 4$ and $b = 5$. Then $9k = 45$, so $k = 5$. Hence they had painted $5(4 + 5)$—i.e., 45—trays that day.

## 86

Say he bought $x$ eggs for 72¢, the price being $\dfrac{864}{x}$¢ per dozen. But $(x + 2)$ eggs for 72¢ would entail the price $\dfrac{864}{x+2}$ ¢ per dozen, so $\dfrac{864}{x} - \dfrac{864}{x+2} = 6.$

Hence $x^2 + 2x - 288 = 0$, i.e., $(x - 16)(x + 18) = 0$ (see Appendix B). So $x = 16$.

He bought 16 eggs @ 54¢ per dozen.

## 87

If the first player threw a 6, the other would be equally likely to throw any one of the six numbers 1 to 6: if the latter threw a 6, neither would have thrown the *higher*. Similarly, if the first threw any one of the other five numbers. So, each throwing once, there would be 36 possible results, all equally probable, but in 6 of them neither player would throw *higher*.

In those 36 results, then, the chance of the first player throwing higher than the other player would be 15 in 36; i.e., 5 in 12. This is appreciably less than "even chances," which would be 5 in 10 or 6 in 12.

## 88

Say a selection of coins was: $X$ 1¢, $Y$ 5¢, $Z$ 10¢, $W$ 25¢, where one or more of $X, Y, Z, W$ can be zero. If there are 10 coins in all, we have $X + 5Y + 10Z + 25W = 51$ and $X + Y + Z + W = 10$, so $4Y + 9Z + 24W = 41$. Then $W = 0$ or 1.

If $W = 0$, then $4Y + 9Z = 41$, with solution $Y = 8$ and $Z = 1$; whence $X = 1$.

If $W = 1$, then $4Y + 9Z = 17$, with solution $Y = 2$ and $Z = 1$; whence $X = 6$.

So there are only two sets of 10 coins each that meet the stated conditions. Sally had more pennies than Stan, so they had:

Sally, 6 1¢, 2 5¢, 1 10¢, 1 25¢; Stan, 1 1¢, 8 5¢, 1 10¢.

### 89

Say *"this"* is $X$. Then *"that"* is $8X$.
So $X + 8X = 3X^2$; hence $3X^2 = 9X$, so $X = 3$.
*"This"* is 3, and *"that"* is 24.

### 90

Say Jake did 3 on west side and $x$ on east side, while Bill did $y$ on west side and $z$ on east side.

Each side had same number of posts, so $x + z = y + 3$     (A)

Jake painted twice as many as Bill, so $x + 3 = 2y + 2z$     (B)

Subtracting (A) from (B), we have $3 - z = y + 2z - 3$; whence $y + 3z = 6$.

Neither $y$ nor $z$ can be zero; hence $y = 3$ and $z = 1$, with $x = 5$.

Bill painted 4 lamp posts.

### 91

Say Ben paid $x$¢ for the jacket, his profit being $(2997 - x)$¢.

Then $\dfrac{100(2997 - x)}{x} = x/3$; whence $x^2 + 300x - 899100 = 0$.

So $(x - 810)(x + 1110) = 0$, hence $x = 810$ (see Appendix B).

Ben paid $8.10 for the jacket.

### 92

When Tony spoke, say it was $X$ minutes after 10:00 p.m.; i.e., $(60 - X)$ minutes before 11:00.

Then, from what he said we have $58 - X = 2(X - 25)$; whence $X = 36$.

The time was 10:36 p.m.

### 93

Say she bought $X$ shirts @ $3 and $X$ @ $1. She spent $4X$ dollars. Then for $2X$ dollars she would have got $2X/3$ shirts @ $3, and $2X$ shirts @ $1. So $2X/3 + 2X = 2X + 4$; whence $X = 6$.

So she bought 12 shirts.

### 94

Say $x$ girls and $y$ boys; so $x^4 = 2y^3$. Then $x$ must be even, so say $x = 2a$; whence $2^3 \times a^4 = y^3$. Then $y$ must be even, so say $y = 2b$, whence $a^4 = b^3$, the general solution of which is $a = m^3$, $b = m^4$. so $x + y = 2m^3 (m + 1)$. But here we have $x + y$ = "near to 50," so $m = 2$, with $x = 16$ and $y = 32$.

Hence there were 16 girls.

### 95

Each having taken $2 in value from their stock of 3 stamps, their respective investments in what remained (i.e., 1 stamp) were in the ratio of $1.50 to 50¢; i.e., 3 to 1.

So they had to share the $3, when that remaining stamp was sold, in the same proportions.

Hence Kim took $2.25 and Ron 75¢.

## 96

Detailed tabulation is advisable here, working back with amounts taken in cents:

|  | Jack | Jill |
|---|---|---|
| They have | $x - 1$ | $y + 1$ |
| If Jill gives Jack 1¢ | $x$ | $y$ |
| If he gives her 1¢ less than half | $\dfrac{2x - y + 2}{2}$ | $\dfrac{3y - 2}{2}$ |
| If she gives him 1¢ less than half | $\dfrac{6x - 3y + 2}{4}$ | $\dfrac{7y - 2x - 2}{4}$ |
| If he gives her 1¢ less than half | $\dfrac{14x - 13y + 14}{8}$ | $\dfrac{21y - 6x - 14}{8}$ |

So

$$\frac{14x - 13y + 14}{8} = \frac{21y - 6x - 14}{8} + 1;$$

whence $17y - 10x = 10$.

This is a simple indeterminate equation (see Appendix C), with the general solution $x = 17k - 1$, $y = 10k$. So $x + y = 27k - 1$.

But their combined wealth is "about 50¢," so $k = 2$, giving $x = 33$ and $y = 20$.

Hence Jack has 32¢ and Jill 21¢.

## 97

Starting with the word "SAL," in the bottom row, we have the sentence. "SAL IS NOW HALF AS OLD AS SUE WAS WHEN SAL WAS A THIRD AS OLD AS SUE IS NOW."

Say Sal's age now is $x$ years, Sue's age $y$ years.

When Sal was $y/3$, Sue was $(4y - 3x)/3$, so $x = (4y - 3x)/6$; whence $9x = 4y$.

Sue is in her teens, and $y$ must be a multiple of 9, so $y = 18$, with $x = 8$.

Sal is 8 years old.

## 98

Say he drove $x$ miles at $(y - 5)$ m.p.h. and then $x$ miles at $(y + 5)$ m.p.h.

Then his total time was $\dfrac{x}{y - 5} + \dfrac{x}{y + 5} = 2$ hours;

whence $x = \dfrac{y^2 - 25}{y}$    (A).

In the first hour, during which he drove *less* than $x$ miles, he drove at $(y - 5)$ m.p.h., so he drove $(y - 5)$ miles.

So in the second hour he drove $(y - 5) + 8$; i.e., $(y + 3)$ miles.

Total distance, then, was $(2y - 2)$ miles; hence $x = y - 1$    (B).

Combining (A) and (B), $y^2 - 25 = y(y - 1)$; whence $y = 25$. Then, $x = 24$.

So he drove a total distance of 48 miles.

## 99

The solution of this problem is by no means simple. It does, however, involve several concepts which apply when solving popular teasers of various types. For this reason the problem itself was included in this little collection, and the solution will be outlined rather fully.

In the three respective lots, say he bought: $x$ @ $x\phi$ for $x^2\phi$, $y$ @ $y\phi$ for $y^2\phi$, and $(260 - x - y)$ @ $(260 - x - y)\phi$ for $(260 - x - y)^2\phi$.

Then $x^2 + y^2 + (260 - x - y)^2 = 26000$; whence $x^2 - (260 - y)x + y^2 - 260y + 20800 = 0$.

Treating this as a quadratic equation in $x$ (see Appendix B), we have $2x = (260 - y) \pm \sqrt{(520y - 15600 - 3y^2)}$.

Then (see Appendix D) $520y - 15600 - 3y^2 = k^2$.

Using the device that was explained in a simpler form in Appendix B, this becomes $(3y - 260)^2 + 3k^2 = 20800$.

A tedious routine of testing would reveal the whole-number values of $y$ and $k$ that will satisfy this equation. However, the working can be greatly reduced if some thought is given to the matter first.

We assume that the smallest of the three lots, unless all three were equal (impossible with total of 260) or unless the two smaller lots were equal, consisted of $y$ shirts. Clearly, then, this must imply $y < 87$; whence $(3y - 260)$ must be negative. Now $(3y - 260)^2 = (260 - 3y)^2$, so we can rewrite the equation as $(260 - 3y)^2 + 3k^2 = 20800$.

$3k^2$ cannot be negative, so $(260 - 3y) < \sqrt{20801}$; hence $y > 39$.

No square number can end with 2, 3, 7, or 8. So, referring to the equation $(260 - 3y)^2 + 3k^2 = 20800$, we can make a tabulation as follows:

| $k^2$ ends with | 0 or 1 or 4 or 5 or 6 or 9. |
|---|---|
| Correspondingly, $3k^2$ ends with | 0    3    2    5    8    7, |
| making $(260 - 3y)^2$ end with | 0    7    8    5    2    3. |

But no square can end with 2, 3, 7, or 8. Hence $(260 - 3y)^2$ must end with 0 or 5; whence $y$ must be a multiple of 5.

So now we have limited the possible values of $y$ to be tested to multiples of 5 that are greater than 38 and less than 87. This final testing can be laid out as:

| $y =$ | 40 | 45 | 50 | . . . | 80 | 85 |
|---|---|---|---|---|---|---|
| $(260 - 3y)^2 =$ | 19600 | 15625 | 12100 | . . . | 400 | 25 |
| $3k^2 =$ | 1200 | 5175 | 8700 | . . . | 20400 | 20775 |
| $k^2 =$ | 400 | 1725 | 2900 | . . . | 6800 | 6925 |
| $k =$ | 20 | — | — | . . . | — | — |

It will be found that whole-number values of both $k$ and $y$ are obtained only where $y = 40$, with $k = 20$.

Going back to the original solution for $x$, then, we

must have $2x = 220 \pm 20$; whence $x = 100$ or $120$.

The three lots, then, contained respectively 40, 100, and 120 shirts. The shirts in the three lots were priced at 40¢, $1.00, and $1.20 each.

## 100

Say the bicycle was worth $X$ dollars.

Then $\dfrac{4(X + 30)}{7} = X + 3$; whence $X = 33$.

The bicycle was worth $33.00.

## 101

No regular units of distance are mentioned, so we say the lengths of their respective steps were:

Ann, $\dfrac{d}{28}$ units; Doug, $\dfrac{d}{24}$ units; and Jack $\dfrac{d}{21}$ units,

where $d$ is the distance in some arbitrary units that Doug covers in 24 steps.

Then for $d = 168$, their respective steps were:

Ann, 6 units; Doug, 7 units; and Jack, 8 units.

So in some particular period of time:

Ann  runs  $6 \times 8 = 48$ units of distance
Doug runs  $7 \times 7 = 49$ units of distance
Jack runs  $8 \times 6 = 48$ units of distance.

Hence Doug must have won the race.

## 102

In each pair the love is mutual.

Mary does not love Bob, so she loves Andy or Charles. But Andy does not love Mary, so Mary must love Charles.

Bob does not want Linda, so he loves Mary or Nan. But Mary is paired off with Charles, so Bob loves Nan.

That leaves Andy and Linda.

The three happy couples are Charles and Mary, Bob and Nan, and Andy and Linda.

### 103

Les had $x$, Stan $y$; the "certain number" was $a$. Then $x + a = 3y - 3a$, and $x - a = 2y + 2a$; whence $3y - 4a = 2y + 3a = x$. So $y = 3a$, with $x = 17a$. Now $x < 26$, and $a$ is a whole number. So $a = 1$; hence $x = 17$ and $y = 3$.

Les had 17 cigarettes.

### 104

Say it cost Kim $X$ cents. Then he made $X^2/100\phi$ profit. So $X^2/100 = 96 - X$; whence $X = 60$ (see Appendix B).

The souvenir cost Kim 60$\phi$.

### 105

$a$ lbs        $b$ lbs

Say the effective weights of the unloaded "pans" and their distances in inches from the fulcrum were as shown in diagram. Then for the unloaded balance $aX = bY$.

Now add $W$, weight of the girl, to each pan in turn, with the corresponding "necessary weight" added to the other pan. This gives, $Y(W + b) = X(a + 64)$ and $Y(100 + b) = X(a + W)$. But $aX = bY$, so we have $YW = 64X$ and $100Y = XW$. Hence $W^2 = 6400$; whence $W = 80$.

The girl weighed 80 pounds.

## 106

Say $X$ took salt alone, $Y$ pepper alone, $Z$ neither, $3Z$ both. Then we have $X + 3Z = 9$ and $Y + 3Z = 11$, so $Y - X = 2$ (see Appendix A).

But $X$ is "some," and $Z$ is "some." Hence from $X + 3Z = 9$, we must have $Z = 2$, with $X = 3$. So $Y = 5$.

3 took salt alone, 5 pepper alone, 2 took neither, 6 took both.

Hence Peter had observed 16 people.

## 107

In one form or other, the basic problem here has puzzled generations of puzzle fans!

When the rock was taken out of the little bowl, that bowl displaced less water, so the water level in the basin fell. It fell by an amount corresponding to the volume of water which would have the same weight as the rock.

When the rock was immersed under water in the basin, it displaced its own volume of water, and the level in the basin rose. The amount it rose, however, corresponded to the volume of the rock—very much less than the volume of an equal weight of water.

Hence this rise of level was less than the previous fall.

So the *net* result was a *fall* in the level of water in the basin.

## 108

Let $X$, $Y$, and $Z$ be the dollars that changed hands between each winner-loser pair in the successive rubbers.

Judy clearly lost $5, so she lost the final rubber with Gwen as partner.

Then we can set up the equations $X + Y - Z = -5$, $X - Y + Z = 29$, and $-X + Y + Z = 25$, which have solution $X = 12$, $Y = 10$, and $Z = 27$ (see Appendix A).

They paid to "nearest 100" at $2, $3, and $6. Re $X$, 6 is a factor of 12 but not of 10 or 27, so the first rubber entailed 200 points at $6. Then the second rubber entailed 500 points at $2, and the third rubber 900 points at $3.

On the third rubber, Sally and Pat each received $27.

### 109

Say $x$ cutlets, $y$ chops. Then $7x + 11y = 94$, with $x$ and $y$ whole numbers. Quick trial gives $x = 4$ and $y = 6$.

The more elegant theoretical solution (see Appendix C) would hardly be justified here with such small numbers.

Button ate 4 cutlets and 6 chops.

### 110

$\frac{5}{7}$ of a pound plus $\frac{5}{7}$ of its weight equaled its complete weight. Hence $\frac{5}{7}$ of a pound equaled $\frac{2}{7}$ of its weight, so 5 pounds would equal twice its weight, and it weighed 2½ pounds.

# ALPHAMETICS

It all started thousands of years ago, probably in ancient China, with puzzles in which the numerals of arithmetical calculations were replaced by letters. In such a puzzle, well known centuries ago as "letter arithmetic" and more recently as a "cryptarithm," each distinct digit was represented by a particular but different letter, the solver being required to reconstruct the original numerical layout.

A very simple example would be:

$$\begin{array}{r} P\,K \\ K\,N \\ \hline K\,N\,K \end{array}$$

In 1955 I coined the new word "alphametic" to designate a more sophisticated and interesting-looking variation on the same general theme. In an alphametic the letters must form meaningful words and phrases, rather than the jumbled array of the cryptarithm. As an alphametic, then, the puzzle shown above could appear as:

$$\begin{array}{r} A\,D \\ D\,I \\ \hline D\,I\,D \end{array} \quad \text{with unique solution} \quad \begin{array}{r} 9\,1 \\ 1\,0 \\ \hline 1\,0\,1 \end{array}$$

This is *meaningful* as referring to an advertisement

89

that Diane produced. Although precisely the same problem arithmetically, the alphametic form is obviously more likely to arouse the interest of ordinary people who might well be repelled by the apparently meaningless "jumbled-letters" form. In fact, the introduction of the alphametic and its acceptance by puzzlemakers throughout the world have led to an amazing spread of popular interest in this form as a pastime that requires only basic arithmetical understanding and sound reasoning for its enjoyment.

In the forty alphametics that follow these introductory remarks, only the main types of simple arithmetical calculations are involved—addition, subtraction, multiplication, division. Alphametics can be constructed, however, based on such more complex operations as calculation of a square root, solution of a differential equation, and others.

Detailed *solutions* for the first five alphametics are given in the Solutions Section, but only the bare *answers* are given for the remainder.

No two alphametics, even of the same type, require the same approach in the solving. It is quite impossible to lay down any specific rules or procedures for solving such puzzles. However, a few observations and hints of a general nature may help the reader who is not very familiar with this fascinating pastime.

The first essential then, having copied the layout on a sheet of paper, is to study the letters of the alphametic and write down any obvious facts regarding their relationships. In doing this, the solver may well adopt a special symbol that can save much space. If we multiply 3 by 4, our product *ends in* 2. Instead of that rather long sentence, precisely the same fact can be noted as "3 $\times$ 4 $\to$ 2." Similarly, 24 $\times$ 19 $\to$ 6, and on exactly similar lines 24 $\times$ 19 $\to$ 56. This is a most useful device, and the *"ends in"* symbol will be seen in the detailed solutions that follow.

Among the facts that may be involved in solving an alphametic, all within the framework of elementary arithmetic, the following are worth noting here.

(*1*)   Say we have one "column" in an addition or subtraction

$$\frac{\begin{matrix} K \\ K \end{matrix}}{K}$$

appearing as —, then we know that K = zero

*or* 9. The possibility that "carry 1" or "borrow 1" is involved must always be remembered in such cases. Obviously much the same situation arises where, in a column of three letters in the body of an addition or subtraction, with two letters the same, the third letter may have to be zero or 9.

(*2*)   No perfect square can end with 2, 3, 7, or 8. For example, say we have (E × E) → T. Then T cannot represent 2, 3, 7, or 8. Also, since $5^2 \to 5$, $6^2 \to 6$, and $1^2 \to 1$, we must immediately be limited right away in this case to the following pairs of values, which would be written down as known facts:

E = 2 3 4 7 8 9
T = 4 9 6 9 4 1

(3)   When carrying out a regular arithmetical calculation, we never write down a *zero* as the *first* digit of a number. Hence in an alphametic, the first letter of a "word" can never stand for zero.

Some of the alphametics that follow will be seen to display asterisks (or similar) as well as regular letters. The asterisks merely indicate the positions of numerals, without relation to their respective values.

Occasionally an alphametic will include one or more numerals in its make-up. In such cases, unless specifically stated to the contrary, this does not mean that no letter in the puzzle can stand for one of those numerals.

The forty alphametics are graded very approximately according to difficulty. None are very difficult, but they all can present a challenge for the diversion of the enthusiastic solver.

## PROBLEMS

```
1. L A B E L          2.    T H E
      A L L                 T E N
    S E A L                 M E N
    ─────────             ─────────
    B A L E S             M E E T
```

3. This alphametic is of particular interest in that the three *words* consist of the same four letters.

```
        S N I P
        N I P S
        ─────────
        P I N S
```

4.
```
      O L D ) C R O W S ( D O
            C U S S
            ─────────
            W U S
            W U S
            ─────────
            ─ ─ ─
```

5. "Is that new?" Tony asked,
   As he strolled through the zoo,
   And the keeper replied:
   "It's not new, it's a gnu."

```
      B I G ) N U G S ( O R
            B I G
            ─────────
            G N U S
            G N U S
            ─────────
            ─ ─ ─ ─
```

```
6. S T A R S           7. S Y S T E M
     R A T E              D E E M E D
   ───────────          ─────────────
   T R E A T              S E N S E
```

8.
```
        I F ) G E N T ( G O
              I F
            ───────
            F I T
            * * *
            ───────
            - - -
```

9.
```
        G E T ) T O G S ( O N
              7 7 7
            ─────────
            B E E S
            * * * *
            ─────────
            - - - -
```

10. 
```
    S L O W
    S L O W
    O L D
    ─────────
    O W L S
```

11.
```
        O I L
        N O
        O I L
        O N
        ───────
        L I N O
```

12.
```
    W H A T
        A
    ─────────
    S H O W
```

13.
```
        H A V E
            7
        ─────────
        C A S E S
```

14.
```
    T R I E D
    R I D E
    ─────────
    S T E E R
```

15.
```
    C R A C K S
    T R A C K S
    ───────────
    R A C K E T
```

**16.**
```
P E T ) S K I R T ( I S
        T H E
        ———
        P E T
        P E T
        ———
        - - -
```

**17.**
```
L I E N ) F I L E D ( S O
          L I E N
          ———
          H E L D
          * * * *
          ———
          - - - -
```

**18.**
```
    P U T
      O N
    ———
    F A T
  N O T
  ———
  F E A T
```

**19.**
```
    S A L
    S E E
    T H E
    S U E Z
  ———
  C A N A L
```

**20.**
```
    M A D
      A S
    ———
    T H E
  M A D
  ———
  M U L E
```

**21.**
```
    Q U I T
    N O W
  ———
    * * * *
  * * * * *
  ———
  T T T T T
```

**22.**
```
    T H R E E
    T H R E E
    T H R E E
  E L E V E N
  ———
  T W E N T Y
```

**23.**
```
Q ) U  A  I  L
  ———
  P ) R  A  Y
    ———
    E ) A  T
      ———
      U  P
```

24.
```
            T U T
            T U T
            -------
          * * * *
        *  W O W
      *  *  *  *
      -----------
      W H I S K Y
```

25.
```
    T I N ) T A C K S ( I N
            T E N T
            -------
            R I P *
          * * * *
          ---------
            * * *
```

26. 
```
    R E A L T O R
      T R A I L S
    -------------
    L O O T E R
```

27.
```
        F I V E
        F I V E
        N I N E
    E L E V E N
    -----------
    T H I R T Y
```

28.
```
    F E W ) D E N Y ( W E
          * * *
          -----
          T R Y
          * * *
          -----
          - - -
```

29.
```
        N I N E
      S E V E N
      S E V E N
      S E V E N
      ---------
      T H I R T Y
```

30.
```
      S I X
      S I X
      ───────
    * * * *
    * * * *
  * * A S
  ───────────
  A D O Z E N
```

31.
```
          I
        D O
      N O T
    K N O W
    ───────────
    T R I C K
```
*Note:* It is a *prime* TRICK.

32. This is a most unusual multiplication alphametic.

As usual, each letter stands for a different figure. The relevant letters comprise the four words printed in capitals, and you only have to answer the question.

"What SENSE does it make, if nine HENS give seven EGGS?"

33.
```
F R O G ) G U L P E D ( F L Y
          * * * *
          ───────────
          * * * * *
          * * * * G
          ───────────
            * * * U *
            * * * P *
            ───────────
              * P *
```

34.
```
S I X ) E L E V E N ( O N E
        * * * *
        ───────────
          * * * *
          * * * *
          ───────────
            * * *
            * * *
            ───────────
              5
```

35.          C O P S
             C L O S E
             C E L L A R
             C O R P S E
               C A S E
             C O L L A R
             ───────────
             R E C T O R

36.          C O U R T
             C L E A R S
             ───────────
             R E C T O R

*Note:* Of course we could not accept an *odd* RECTOR! What must the REC-TOR be?

37.          A F T E R
             R E C T O R
             F R E E D
             C U R A T E
             ───────────
             A C C U S E D

38.          C U R A T E
               C A S E
             S E C U R E
             ───────────
             R E M A N D

*Note:* Indeed an *odd* CASE!

39.          W E A R Y
             L A W Y E R
             R E A L L Y
             ───────────
             Y A W N E D

40.          C E L L A R
             M U R D E R
             C L E R I C
             ───────────
             C L E A R E D

## SOLUTIONS

**1. L A B E L**   This is obviously a matter of ad-
   **A L L**   dition, and B = L + 1.
   **S E A L**   So we had "carry 1" from A + S.
   ──────   Then, S + "carry from BAE" = 10.
   **B A L E S**   But that "carry" cannot exceed 2,
   so S = 8 or 9.

We now tabulate the values of L and other letters, corresponding to those alternative values for S. Wherever an unacceptable value for any letter may arise, such as a duplication or a contradictory value, we strike it out.

$$S = \quad 8 \quad 9$$
$$3L \to S, \quad \text{so } L = \quad 6 \quad 3$$
$$\text{with "carry"} = \quad 1 \quad 0$$

$$L + A + \text{"carry"} = 10, \quad \text{so } A = \quad 3 \quad 7$$
$$\text{with "carry"} = \quad 1 \quad 1$$

$$B + A + E + \text{"carry 1"} \quad\quad\quad = 26 \quad 13$$
$$L + A + E + \text{"carry 1"} \quad\quad\quad = 25 \quad 12$$
$$L + A + \text{"carry 1"} \quad\quad\quad\quad\quad = 10 \quad 11$$

$$\text{So } E = \cancel{15} \quad 1$$

There remains the one acceptable set of values, with S = 9. So we have:

```
            3 7 4 1 3
              7 3 3
            9 1 7 3
            ─────────
            4 7 3 1 9
```

2.  T H E     Considering the column HEE, it is
    T E N     seen that H + E + "carry from
    M E N     ENN" = 10.
    ───────       Hence, there must be "carry, 1" to
    M E E T   the TTM column, giving $2T + M + 1 \to E$, with M = 1 or 2.

Taking that a stage further, $2T + M + 1 = 10M + E$, hence $2T = E + 9M - 1$, with M = 1 or 2. 2T must be even. So, if M = 1, E must be even; if M = 2, E is odd.

We now tabulate for possible values of E and M, with corresponding values of T and the other two letters. Where an unacceptable value arises, we strike it out.

| E = | 0 | 2 | 4 | 6 | 8 | 1 |
|-----|---|---|---|---|---|---|
| M = | 1 | 1 | 1 | 1 | 1 | 2 |
| T = | 4 | 5 | 6 | 7 | $\cancel{8}$ | 9 |

| From ENN, | $2N \to$ | 4 | $\cancel{5}$ | 2 | $\cancel{1}$ | - | 8 |
|-----------|----------|---|---|---|---|---|---|
|           | N = | 2 | 7 | - | - | - | 4 |

| "Carry" from EEN = | 0 | 1 | - | - | - | 0 |
|--------------------|---|---|---|---|---|---|
| Then,     H + E = | 10 | 9 | - | - | - | 10 |
| making      H = | - | 9 | - | - | - | $\cancel{0}$ |

There remains only the one set of acceptable values, so we have:

$$
\begin{array}{r}
4\ 9\ 0 \\
4\ 0\ 7 \\
1\ 0\ 7 \\
\hline
1\ 0\ 0\ 4
\end{array}
$$

3.  S N I P    If this were an addition, we would
    N I P S    have P = zero. This is impossible,
    ———        since P is the first letter of PINS.
    P I N S    Hence it must be a subtraction.

From S — N, S > P. Also, S + S → P, so 2S = P + 10, which gives P = 2S — 10, with S > 5.

From I — P, we have P + N → I — 1. But, from S — N, S = P + N or S = P + N + 1. The latter would entail S = I, so we must have S = P + N, which gives N = S — P, so N = 10 — S.

We had P + N → I — 1; whence I → P + N + 1, so I → S + 1. Now S > 5. If I = S + 1, then we would have I > 6, in which case "N — I" would entail *borrowing*, leading to S = N + P + 1, which has been proved unacceptable. Hence we must have I = S — 9.

We now have P, N, and I all in terms of S:

P = 2S — 10    N = 10 — S    I = S — 9

Since I = S — 9, we must have S = 9, with I = zero, P = 8, N = 1. So the complete subtraction is

$$
\begin{array}{r}
9\ 1\ 0\ 8 \\
1\ 0\ 8\ 9 \\
\hline
8\ 0\ 1\ 9
\end{array}
$$

4.  O L D ) C R O W S ( D O    From RO — US,
      C U S S                 we have R = U +
      ———                     1, so U < 9 and, S
      W U S                   > O.
      W U S                       OLD × O gives a
      ———                     three-digit product,
      — — —                   and O > 1; hence
                              O = 2 or 3. Also,
                              D > O.

If D = 3, then O = 2, which would make "OLD × D" a three-digit product.

So D > 3. Also, D × D → S, and S > O, so D cannot be 9.

We now tabulate possible values of D and S, with the alternative values for O and corresponding other values. Where an unacceptable value arises, we strike it out.

| | D = | 4 | | 7 | | 8 | |
|---|---|---|---|---|---|---|---|
| | S = | 6 | | 9 | | 4 | |
| | O = | 2 | 3 | 2 | 3 | 2 | 3 |
| W equals at least O², so | | | | | | | |
| from O — S | W = | 5 | – | – | – | 7 | 9 |
| Then | OW = | 25 | – | – | – | 27 | 39 |
| and | SS = | 66 | – | – | – | 44 | 44 |
| making | WU = | 5̶9̶ | – | – | – | 8̶3̶ | 95 |

There remains only the one set of acceptable values, with WUS = 954, and O = 3. So OLD = 318. Also, since U = 5, we have R = 6. Then, because 318 × 8 starts with 2, C = 2. So we have:

```
3 1 8 ) 2 6 3 9 4 ( 8 3
        2 5 4 4

          9 5 4
          9 5 4

          – – –
```

5. B I G ) N U G S ( O R    Obviously, O = 1,
      B I G        and U = zero.
      ———        So I > U; hence
      G N U S     N = B + G + 1.
      G N U S     Because BIG × R
      ———        = GNUS, B > G.
      – – – –     Because U = zero,

I + N = 10.
B + G > 4, so N > 5.

We now tabulate possible values of N and I, with corresponding values of the other letters complying with the facts already noted. Where a duplication or other clearly unacceptable value arises, we strike out as necessary.

|        |       |   |   |   |
|--------|-------|---|---|---|
|        | N =   | 6 | 7 | 8 |
|        | I =   | 4 | 3 | 2 |
| with   | B =   | 3 | 4 | 4 |
| and    | G =   | 2 | 2 | 3 |
| making | GNUS = | 260S | 270S | 380S |
| and    | BIG = | 342 | 432 | 423 |
| Dividing, | R = | 7 | 6 | 9 |
| Then,  | G × R → S = | 4̸ | 2̸ | 7 |

There remaining only the one set of acceptable values, we have:

```
423 ) 8 0 3 7 ( 1 9
      4 2 3
      ─────
      3 8 0 7
      3 8 0 7
      ─────
      ─ ─ ─ ─
```

6. $89568 + 6591 = 96159.$
7. $939042 - 844248 = 94794.$
8. $87 ) 1653 ( 19$
9. $259 ) 9324 ( 36$
10. $2147 + 2147 + 418 = 4712.$
11. $761 + 87 + 761 + 78 = 1687.$
12. $4027 \times 2 = 8054.$
13. $6531 \times 7 = 45717.$
14. $36879 + 6897 = 43776.$
15. $587506 + 287506 = 875012.$
16. $489 ) 10269 ( 21$
17. $4873 ) 58476 ( 12$
18. $130 \times 56 = 7280.$
19. $920 + 977 + 547 + 9876 = 12320.$
20. $219 \times 13 = 2847$
21. $1365 \times 407 = 555555$ (*Clue:* Factors of 111111).
22. $73544 + 73544 + 73544 + 494046 = 714678.$
23.
```
   5 ) 1   9   6   0
       4 ) 3   9   2
           7 ) 9   8
               1   4
```
24. $929 \times 929 = 863041.$
25. $397 ) 38640 ( 97$

26. 1548731 — 714980 = 833751.
27. 4027 + 4027 + 5057 + 797275 = 810386.
28. 142 ) 3408 ( 24
29. 3239 + 49793 + 49793 + 49793 = 152618.
30. 567 × 567 = 321489.
31. 7 + 25 + 851 + 9856 = 10739 (a prime number).
32. SENSE = 58258 (6825 × 9 = 8775 × 7).
33. 2105 ) 587436 ( 279
34. 573 ) 161018 ( 281
35. 2730 + 29704 + 249918 + 278304 + 2104 + 279918 = 842678.
36. RECTOR = 817368 (even) = 76083 + 741285, with 2 and 0 interchangeable.
37. 18029 + 927069 + 89225 + 739102 = 1773425.
38. 398027 + 3047 + 473987 = 875061 (3047 is odd).
39. 81729 + 678912 + 217669 = 978310.
40. 102263 + 983703 + 120341 = 1206307.

# APPENDICES

## APPENDIX A

The simplest type of equation is called a *linear equation.*

Mentally, and probably without realizing that they are doing so, most people solve equations of this type every day. Maybe you bought seven pears for sixty-three cents. What did each cost? "In your head," you divided 63 by 7, deriving 9¢ per pear. In fact, you virtually said $7X = 63$, so $X = 63/7 = 9$.

Where we have two (or three or more) equations of this type, all applying simultaneously, the operation is not quite so simple.

Say we have $5X + 3Y = 36$ and $2X + 7Y = 55$. The standard approach to such a "pair of simultaneous equations" is to eliminate $X$ or $Y$, as shown here:

Multiplying the first by 2, we derive

$$10X + 6Y = 72.$$

Multiplying the second by 5, we derive

$$10X + 35Y = 275.$$

Subtracting one from the other,

$$29Y = 203.$$
$$Y = 7.$$

Then, from the first equation, we have

$$5X = 36 - 21 = 15,$$
$$X = 3.$$

so

It will be noted that we can multiply each side of an equation by the same number without destroying the equality. So in this case we chose to multiply each side of one equation by 2, and each side of the other by 5, in order to arrive at identical coefficients for $X$ (i.e., 10): that enabled us to eliminate the $X$ terms by subtraction.

The same principle is used in solving a system of three or more simultaneous equations. For example, say we have:

$$\left. \begin{array}{l} 2X + 3Y - 2Z = 15 \\ 3X + \phantom{3}Y + \phantom{3}Z = 16 \\ \phantom{3}X + 4Y + 3Z = 19 \end{array} \right\} \begin{array}{l} (A) \\ (B) \\ (C) \end{array}$$

Here it will be convenient to eliminate the $Z$ terms first.

Multiplying equation (B) by 2 and by 3, we can set up two pairs of valid equations:

$$\left. \begin{array}{l} 2X + 3Y - 2Z = 15 \\ 6X + 2Y + 2Z = 32 \end{array} \right\}$$

Eliminating $Z$,    $8X + 5Y \phantom{+ 3Z} = 47$

and

$$\left. \begin{array}{l} 9X + 3Y + 3Z = 48 \\ \phantom{9}X + 4Y + 3Z = 19 \end{array} \right\}$$

Eliminating $Z$,    $8X - \phantom{5}Y \phantom{+ 3Z} = 29$

Now we have the pair of simultaneous equations:

$$\left. \begin{array}{l} 8X + 5Y = 47 \\ 8X - \phantom{5}Y = 29 \end{array} \right\}$$

Eliminating $X$,    $6Y = 18$; whence $Y = 3$.

Then, substituting this value for $Y$, we have $8X = 32$, so $X = 4$.

Finally, we substitute these values for $X$ and $Y$, in equation (B), to derive $Z = 16 - 12 - 3 = 1$. So $X = 4, Y = 3, Z = 1$.

## APPENDIX B

A *quadratic equation* involves the square of the "unknown."

The standard solution for this type of equation, derived in detail and proved in any elementary

algebra textbook, is not difficult to remember:
If $ax^2 - bx + c = 0$, then $2ax = b \pm \sqrt{b^2 - 4ac}$.

In many cases, however, a rather different approach is preferable, although it of course leads to the same ultimate result. This entails no formula to be remembered and should be quite easy to understand from a couple of numerical examples. It will be seen that we manipulate the equation as necessary in order to transform it into a new equation of form $X^2 = Y$, which must have two solutions: $X = + \sqrt{Y}$ and $X = - \sqrt{Y}$.

Say we have $x^2 + x - 12 = 0$. Multiplying by 4, this becomes $4x^2 + 4x - 48 = 0$, which can be shown as $4x^2 + 4x + 1 = 49$. Then $(2x + 1)^2 = 49$, so $2x + 1 = \pm 7$; whence $x = 3$ or $x = - 4$.

In a more complex example, say $3x^2 - 19x - 14 = 0$, multiplying by 12, this becomes $36x^2 - 228x - 168 = 0$, which can be shown as $36x^2 - 228x + 361 = 529$. Then $(6x - 19)^2 = 529$, so $6x - 19 = \pm 23$; whence $x = 7$ or $x = - 2/3$.

## APPENDIX C

Many popular teasers depend on the solution of what is called a *simple indeterminate equation,* a very simple example of which would be the equation $7X - 3Y = 11$ with the stipulation that $X$ and $Y$ must both be whole numbers.

That *whole number* condition is inherent in such equations, and is vital in solving them.

Say we wish to solve $7X - 3Y = 11$, where $X$ and $Y$ are both whole numbers.

Since 3 is the smaller of the two coefficients, we divide through by 3:

$$2X + \frac{X}{3} - Y = 4 - \frac{1}{3}$$

which becomes $\qquad \dfrac{X + 1}{3} = Y - 2X + 4$

Now $(Y - 2X + 4)$ must be a whole number, so $\dfrac{X + 1}{3}$ must also be a whole number.

Say $\dfrac{X + 1}{3} = k$, where $k$ is some unspecified whole number (positive, negative, or even zero). Then $X = 3k - 1$.

Substituting this value for $X$ in the original equation, we have $3Y = 21k - 18$; whence $Y = 7k - 6$.

The general solution, then, is $X = 3k - 1$, $Y = 7k - 6$.

By giving any desired whole-number value to $k$, we will obtain a particular numerical solution to the original equation. For example, with $k = 2$, we have $X = 5$, $Y = 8$.

Where a popular teaser involves solution of such an equation, there will be some extra condition to pinpoint the required particular solution among the infinite number of possible whole-number solutions. In our example, we might have some stipulation that required $Y$ to be "in the thirties"; then we should have to set $k = 6$, giving $X = 17$, $Y = 36$.

This was a very simple example. When we divided through by 3, the coefficient of $Y$, we obtained the fraction of $X$ as $X/3$: a fraction with unity as numerator (as opposed to $2X/3$, say).

So now we consider a slightly more complex case, taking the equation $11X - 7Y = 2$.

Dividing through by 7, the smaller coefficient as before, we have $X + \dfrac{4X}{7} - Y = \dfrac{2}{7}$; whence $\dfrac{4X - 2}{7}$ is a whole number, so $\dfrac{2(2X - 1)}{7}$ is a whole number. Then $\dfrac{2X - 1}{7}$ must be a whole number.

Here we do not have unity as the coefficient of $X$ in the numerator of the fraction, so we must take a further step to arrive at that necessary situation.

If we multiply a whole number by any whole number, the result will be a whole number. So we multiply by a selected whole number, such that the new coefficient of $X$ will be "1 more" (or "1 less") than a multiple of 7. For this we select 4 as our multiplier.

Multiplying by 4, $\dfrac{2X - 1}{7}$ becomes $\dfrac{8X - 4}{7}$, which will also be a whole number. That, in turn, becomes $X + \dfrac{X - 4}{7}$, which implies that $\dfrac{X - 4}{7}$ must be a whole number.

Now we have unity as the coefficient of $X$ in the numerator, so we can say $\dfrac{X - 4}{7} = k$; whence $X = 7k + 4$. Then, substituting this value for $X$ in the original equation (i.e., $11X - 7Y = 2$), we derive $Y = 11k + 6$.

The required general solution, then, is $X = 7k + 4$, $Y = 11k + 6$.

If some condition stipulated that $X$ in this case must be between 40 and 50, we would have to set $k = 6$, giving $X = 46$, $Y = 72$.

The selection of the right *multiplier* is sometimes far from easy (in this last example, 4 could be picked at sight). In such cases it may have to be found by a process of trial, bearing in mind the desired result. There is a standard method for calculating what the *multiplier* should be, without trial and error, and this will be found in textbooks, but the principles involved are somewhat outside the scope of this book.

## APPENDIX D

Many of the more difficult popular teasers entail the solving of what are called *second-degree indeterminate equations,* which may be described more simply as indeterminate equations that involve squares. A simple example is $3x^2 + 2xy - y^2 = 15$, in which, as in all indeterminate equations, we are concerned only with whole-number values of $x$ and $y$.

We take that example, writing it as $3x^2 + 2yx - y^2 - 15 = 0$, and treat this as an ordinary quadratic equation in $x$ (see Appendix B).

Then    $6x = -2y \pm \sqrt{4y^2 + 12y^2 + 180}$;

whence    $3x = -y \pm \sqrt{4y^2 + 45}$    (A)

Since whole-number values are required, the expression under the square-root sign must be a perfect square. This, or some similar requirement, is basic in the solution of most second-degree indeterminate equations.

So say $4y^2 + 45 = k^2$, whence $k$ is some unspecified whole number.

Then $k^2 - (2y)^2 = 45$; whence $(k + 2y)(k - 2y) = 45$.

We now tabulate, bringing in the possible pairs of factors of 45, but observing that with a positive value of $y$ we must have $(k + 2y)$ greater than $(k - 2y)$, for negative values are unlikely to be called for in a popular teaser.

| $k + 2y =$ | 45 | 15 | 9 |
|---|---|---|---|
| $k - 2y =$ | 1 | 3 | 5 |

adding gives

| $k$ = | 23 | 9 | 7 |
|---|---|---|---|

subtracting gives

| $y$ = | 11 | 3 | 1 |
|---|---|---|---|

from (A)

| $3x$ = | 12 or −34 | 6 or −12 | 6 or −8 |
|---|---|---|---|

whence

| $x$ = | 4 | — | 2 or −4 | 3 | — |
|---|---|---|---|---|---|

We disregarded fractional values of $x$ in the last line of the tabulation. Assuming we seek only positive values for $x$ and $y$, we have found that there are three acceptable solutions:

$x = 4, y = 11$;   $x = 2, y = 3$;   $x = 2, y = 1$.

We now take a rather less simple example, in which the same principles will be seen to apply.

Say $x^2 - 3xy - 7y = 11$, both $x$ and $y$ being positive.

Then $x^2 - 3yx - 7y - 11 = 0$, which has solution in $x$:

$$2x = 3y \pm \sqrt{(9y^2 + 28y + 44)} \quad \text{(B)}$$

So $9y^2 + 28y + 44 = k^2$ (compare with previous example),

and $81y^2 + 252y + 396 = 9k^2$; hence $(9y + 14)^2 + 200 = 9k^2$,

so $(3k)^2 - (9y + 14)^2 = 200$.

Here $(9y + 14)$ must obviously be positive, so we tabulate for three alternative pairs of factors of 200; i.e., $[3k + (9y + 14)] [3k - (9y + 14)] = 100 \times 2$, or $50 \times 4$, or $20 \times 10$.

Carrying through the tabulation procedure, as in the previous example, and using the solution given in (B), only one acceptable solution will be found in positive whole numbers: $x = 6$, $y = 1$.

It should be noted that in both examples we arrived at a final stage with a modified equation in the form $X^2 - Y^2 = m$, where $m$ is a whole number.

In almost all second-degree indeterminate equations the solution depends on deriving a modified equation in the form $X^2 \pm eY^2 = m$. In the two examples already considered, the $e$ was unity and the minus sign applied. In many cases, the $e$ will be some whole number other than unity, with either plus or minus sign, and the whole number $m$ may be negative; for example; $(x + 1)^2 + 2k^2 = 83$, $(2y - 3)^2 - 3k^2 = -83$, etc.

This brief introduction, however, can be no place for further discussion of those and other more complex cases: they are all covered in detail in textbooks, and some special aspects are discussed at length in *Mathematical Diversions,* by J. A. H. Hunter and J. S. Madachy. What has been outlined here may have introduced the reader to the general principles that are involved in dealing with second-degree indeterminate equations.

## APPENDIX E

Some inferential problems may be solved neatly by using the ideas of *Boolean algebra,* which is the basis of the mathematics of logic. Only three problems of this general type appear in this book and in fact all three can be solved very simply by conventional methods as outlined in the "answers" section, but a brief outline of the Boolean approach may be of interest.

We adopt the convention that something "true" has the value 1, and something "false" the value 0. Using code symbols for the "somethings" we can form expressions and equations that may be treated much the same as those in normal algebra.

A very simple example will show how the method is used. Say we have two statements about the name of a girl: one says "Betty Price," the other "Gwen Price," and we are told that each contains one mistake. Then obviously Price is her family name, and her first name is neither Betty nor Gwen.

Now let us see how this could have been handled by Boolean algebra. We have only two numerical values, 0 and 1. There's nothing more true than true: if in our working we derive a number greater than unity we must construe it as unity.

Let $B$ stand for Betty, $G$ for Gwen, $P$ for Price. Then represent each statement in two ways:

*Multiplication:* If both $B$ and $P$ equal 1 (both true), then the product $BP = 1$. But if either $B$ or $P$ equals zero (either is false), then $BP = 0$.

*Addition:* If either $B$ or $P$ (or both) equals 1, then $B + P = 1$.

So we say,

$$(B + P)(G + P) = 1 \times 1 = 1, \text{ whence}$$
$$BG + BP + GP + P^2 = 1.$$

But, $BP = 0$ and $GP = 0$, and obviously $BG = 0$, so $P^2 = 1$, whence $P = 1$. Her surname is Price.

Let us see how these ideas could apply to the problem of the broken window, No. 45. There were four children, one being the culprit. We establish a suitable code: John $= J$, Gail $= G$, Sally $= S$, Ann $= A$. The four statements may be coded as follows—Ann's: $J$; John's: $G$; Sally's: $(J + G + A)$; Gail's: $(J + S + A)$.

Only one spoke the truth, so $(A + J + G)$ $(A + J + S) = 0$, hence $A^2 + AJ + AS + AJ + J^2 + JS + GA + GJ + GS = 0$. Each of the 2-letter terms, such as $AJ$, must equal zero, so we are left with $A^2 + J^2 = 0$, hence $A + J = 0$. So neither Ann nor John was guilty, which makes Gail or Sally guilty: i.e., $G + S = 1$. But, if $G = 1$, both John and Sally must have spoken the truth. So $S = 1$, and Sally was the culprit.

A CATALOG OF SELECTED
# DOVER BOOKS
IN ALL FIELDS OF INTEREST

# A CATALOG OF SELECTED DOVER BOOKS IN ALL FIELDS OF INTEREST

DRAWINGS OF REMBRANDT, edited by Seymour Slive. Updated Lippmann, Hofstede de Groot edition, with definitive scholarly apparatus. All portraits, biblical sketches, landscapes, nudes. Oriental figures, classical studies, together with selection of work by followers. 550 illustrations. Total of 630pp. 9⅛ × 12¼.
21485-0, 21486-9 Pa., Two-vol. set $29.90

GHOST AND HORROR STORIES OF AMBROSE BIERCE, Ambrose Bierce. 24 tales vividly imagined, strangely prophetic, and decades ahead of their time in technical skill: "The Damned Thing," "An Inhabitant of Carcosa," "The Eyes of the Panther," "Moxon's Master," and 20 more. 199pp. 5⅜ × 8½. 20767-6 Pa. $3.95

ETHICAL WRITINGS OF MAIMONIDES, Maimonides. Most significant ethical works of great medieval sage, newly translated for utmost precision, readability. Laws Concerning Character Traits, Eight Chapters, more. 192pp. 5⅜ × 8½.
24522-5 Pa. $4.50

THE EXPLORATION OF THE COLORADO RIVER AND ITS CANYONS, J. W. Powell. Full text of Powell's 1,000-mile expedition down the fabled Colorado in 1869. Superb account of terrain, geology, vegetation, Indians, famine, mutiny, treacherous rapids, mighty canyons, during exploration of last unknown part of continental U.S. 400pp. 5⅜ × 8½. 20094-9 Pa. $7.95

HISTORY OF PHILOSOPHY, Julián Marías. Clearest one-volume history on the market. Every major philosopher and dozens of others, to Existentialism and later. 505pp. 5⅜ × 8½. 21739-6 Pa. $9.95

ALL ABOUT LIGHTNING, Martin A. Uman. Highly readable non-technical survey of nature and causes of lightning, thunderstorms, ball lightning, St. Elmo's Fire, much more. Illustrated. 192pp. 5⅜ × 8½. 25237-X Pa. $5.95

SAILING ALONE AROUND THE WORLD, Captain Joshua Slocum. First man to sail around the world, alone, in small boat. One of great feats of seamanship told in delightful manner. 67 illustrations. 294pp. 5⅜ × 8½. 20326-3 Pa. $4.95

LETTERS AND NOTES ON THE MANNERS, CUSTOMS AND CONDITIONS OF THE NORTH AMERICAN INDIANS, George Catlin. Classic account of life among Plains Indians: ceremonies, hunt, warfare, etc. 312 plates. 572pp. of text. 6⅛ × 9¼. 22118-0, 22119-9, Pa. Two-vol. set $17.90

ALASKA: The Harriman Expedition, 1899, John Burroughs, John Muir, et al. Informative, engrossing accounts of two-month, 9,000-mile expedition. Native peoples, wildlife, forests, geography, salmon industry, glaciers, more. Profusely illustrated. 240 black-and-white line drawings. 124 black-and-white photographs. 3 maps. Index. 576pp. 5⅜ × 8½. 25109-8 Pa. $11.95

HOW TO WRITE, Gertrude Stein. Gertrude Stein claimed anyone could understand her unconventional writing—here are clues to help. Fascinating improvisations, language experiments, explanations illuminate Stein's craft and the art of writing. Total of 414pp. 4⅜ × 6⅜. 23144-5 Pa. $6.95

ADVENTURES AT SEA IN THE GREAT AGE OF SAIL: Five Firsthand Narratives, edited by Elliot Snow. Rare true accounts of exploration, whaling, shipwreck, fierce natives, trade, shipboard life, more. 33 illustrations. Introduction. 353pp. 5⅜ × 8½. 25177-2 Pa. $8.95

THE HERBAL OR GENERAL HISTORY OF PLANTS, John Gerard. Classic descriptions of about 2,850 plants—with over 2,700 illustrations—includes Latin and English names, physical descriptions, varieties, time and place of growth, more. 2,706 illustrations. xlv + 1,678pp. 8½ × 12¼. 23147-X Cloth. $75.00

DOROTHY AND THE WIZARD IN OZ, L. Frank Baum. Dorothy and the Wizard visit the center of the Earth, where people are vegetables, glass houses grow and Oz characters reappear. Classic sequel to *Wizard of Oz*. 256pp. 5⅜ × 8. 24714-7 Pa. $5.95

SONGS OF EXPERIENCE: Facsimile Reproduction with 26 Plates in Full Color, William Blake. This facsimile of Blake's original "Illuminated Book" reproduces 26 full-color plates from a rare 1826 edition. Includes "The Tyger," "London," "Holy Thursday," and other immortal poems. 26 color plates. Printed text of poems. 48pp. 5¼ × 7. 24636-1 Pa. $3.50

SONGS OF INNOCENCE, William Blake. The first and most popular of Blake's famous "Illuminated Books," in a facsimile edition reproducing all 31 brightly colored plates. Additional printed text of each poem. 64pp. 5¼ × 7. 22764-2 Pa. $3.50

PRECIOUS STONES, Max Bauer. Classic, thorough study of diamonds, rubies, emeralds, garnets, etc.: physical character, occurrence, properties, use, similar topics. 20 plates, 8 in color. 94 figures. 659pp. 6⅛ × 9¼. 21910-0, 21911-9 Pa., Two-vol. set $15.90

ENCYCLOPEDIA OF VICTORIAN NEEDLEWORK, S. F. A. Caulfeild and Blanche Saward. Full, precise descriptions of stitches, techniques for dozens of needlecrafts—most exhaustive reference of its kind. Over 800 figures. Total of 679pp. 8⅛ × 11. Two volumes. Vol. 1 22800-2 Pa. $11.95
Vol. 2 22801-0 Pa. $11.95

THE MARVELOUS LAND OF OZ, L. Frank Baum. Second Oz book, the Scarecrow and Tin Woodman are back with hero named Tip, Oz magic. 136 illustrations. 287pp. 5⅜ × 8½. 20692-0 Pa. $5.95

WILD FOWL DECOYS, Joel Barber. Basic book on the subject, by foremost authority and collector. Reveals history of decoy making and rigging, place in American culture, different kinds of decoys, how to make them, and how to use them. 140 plates. 156pp. 7⅞ × 10¾. 20011-6 Pa. $8.95

HISTORY OF LACE, Mrs. Bury Palliser. Definitive, profusely illustrated chronicle of lace from earliest times to late 19th century. Laces of Italy, Greece, England, France, Belgium, etc. Landmark of needlework scholarship. 266 illustrations. 672pp. 6⅛ × 9¼. 24742-2 Pa. $14.95

THE BLUE FAIRY BOOK, Andrew Lang. The first, most famous collection, with many familiar tales: Little Red Riding Hood, Aladdin and the Wonderful Lamp, Puss in Boots, Sleeping Beauty, Hansel and Gretel, Rumpelstiltskin; 37 in all. 138 illustrations. 390pp. 5⅜ × 8½. 21437-0 Pa. $6.95

THE STORY OF THE CHAMPIONS OF THE ROUND TABLE, Howard Pyle. Sir Launcelot, Sir Tristram and Sir Percival in spirited adventures of love and triumph retold in Pyle's inimitable style. 50 drawings, 31 full-page. xviii + 329pp. 6½ × 9¼. 21883-X Pa. $7.95

AUDUBON AND HIS JOURNALS, Maria Audubon. Unmatched two-volume portrait of the great artist, naturalist and author contains his journals, an excellent biography by his granddaughter, expert annotations by the noted ornithologist, Dr. Elliott Coues, and 37 superb illustrations. Total of 1,200pp. 5⅜ × 8.

Vol. I 25143-8 Pa. $8.95
Vol. II 25144-6 Pa. $8.95

GREAT DINOSAUR HUNTERS AND THEIR DISCOVERIES, Edwin H. Colbert. Fascinating, lavishly illustrated chronicle of dinosaur research, 1820's to 1960. Achievements of Cope, Marsh, Brown, Buckland, Mantell, Huxley, many others. 384pp. 5¼ × 8¼. 24701-5 Pa. $7.95

THE TASTEMAKERS, Russell Lynes. Informal, illustrated social history of American taste 1850's–1950's. First popularized categories Highbrow, Lowbrow, Middlebrow. 129 illustrations. New (1979) afterword. 384pp. 6 × 9.

23993-4 Pa. $8.95

DOUBLE CROSS PURPOSES, Ronald A. Knox. A treasure hunt in the Scottish Highlands, an old map, unidentified corpse, surprise discoveries keep reader guessing in this cleverly intricate tale of financial skullduggery. 2 black-and-white maps. 320pp. 5⅜ × 8½. (Available in U.S. only) 25032-6 Pa. $6.95

AUTHENTIC VICTORIAN DECORATION AND ORNAMENTATION IN FULL COLOR: 46 Plates from "Studies in Design," Christopher Dresser. Superb full-color lithographs reproduced from rare original portfolio of a major Victorian designer. 48pp. 9¼ × 12¼. 25083-0 Pa. $7.95

PRIMITIVE ART, Franz Boas. Remains the best text ever prepared on subject, thoroughly discussing Indian, African, Asian, Australian, and, especially, North-ern American primitive art. Over 950 illustrations show ceramics, masks, totem poles, weapons, textiles, paintings, much more. 376pp. 5⅜ × 8. 20025-6 Pa. $7.95

SIDELIGHTS ON RELATIVITY, Albert Einstein. Unabridged republication of two lectures delivered by the great physicist in 1920–21. *Ether and Relativity* and *Geometry and Experience*. Elegant ideas in non-mathematical form, accessible to intelligent layman. vi + 56pp. 5⅜ × 8½. 24511-X Pa. $2.95

THE WIT AND HUMOR OF OSCAR WILDE, edited by Alvin Redman. More than 1,000 ripostes, paradoxes, wisecracks: Work is the curse of the drinking classes, I can resist everything except temptation, etc. 258pp. 5⅜ × 8½. 20602-5 Pa. $4.95

ADVENTURES WITH A MICROSCOPE, Richard Headstrom. 59 adventures with clothing fibers, protozoa, ferns and lichens, roots and leaves, much more. 142 illustrations. 232pp. 5⅜ × 8½. 23471-1 Pa. $3.95

AMERICAN CLIPPER SHIPS: 1833–1858, Octavius T. Howe & Frederick C. Matthews. Fully-illustrated, encyclopedic review of 352 clipper ships from the period of America's greatest maritime supremacy. Introduction. 109 halftones. 5 black-and-white line illustrations. Index. Total of 928pp. 5⅜ × 8½.
25115-2, 25116-0 Pa., Two-vol. set $17.90

TOWARDS A NEW ARCHITECTURE, Le Corbusier. Pioneering manifesto by great architect, near legendary founder of "International School." Technical and aesthetic theories, views on industry, economics, relation of form to function, "mass-production spirit," much more. Profusely illustrated. Unabridged translation of 13th French edition. Introduction by Frederick Etchells. 320pp. 6⅛ × 9¼. (Available in U.S. only) 25023-7 Pa. $8.95

THE BOOK OF KELLS, edited by Blanche Cirker. Inexpensive collection of 32 full-color, full-page plates from the greatest illuminated manuscript of the Middle Ages, painstakingly reproduced from rare facsimile edition. Publisher's Note. Captions. 32pp. 9⅜ × 12¼. 24345-1 Pa. $4.95

BEST SCIENCE FICTION STORIES OF H. G. WELLS, H. G. Wells. Full novel *The Invisible Man*, plus 17 short stories: "The Crystal Egg," "Aepyornis Island," "The Strange Orchid," etc. 303pp. 5⅜ × 8½. (Available in U.S. only)
21531-8 Pa. $6.95

AMERICAN SAILING SHIPS: Their Plans and History, Charles G. Davis. Photos, construction details of schooners, frigates, clippers, other sailcraft of 18th to early 20th centuries—plus entertaining discourse on design, rigging, nautical lore, much more. 137 black-and-white illustrations. 240pp. 6⅛ × 9¼.
24658-2 Pa. $6.95

ENTERTAINING MATHEMATICAL PUZZLES, Martin Gardner. Selection of author's favorite conundrums involving arithmetic, money, speed, etc., with lively commentary. Complete solutions. 112pp. 5⅜ × 8½. 25211-6 Pa. $2.95

THE WILL TO BELIEVE, HUMAN IMMORTALITY, William James. Two books bound together. Effect of irrational on logical, and arguments for human immortality. 402pp. 5⅜ × 8½. 20291-7 Pa. $7.95

THE HAUNTED MONASTERY and THE CHINESE MAZE MURDERS, Robert Van Gulik. 2 full novels by Van Gulik continue adventures of Judge Dee and his companions. An evil Taoist monastery, seemingly supernatural events; overgrown topiary maze that hides strange crimes. Set in 7th-century China. 27 illustrations. 328pp. 5⅜ × 8½. 23502-5 Pa. $6.95

CELEBRATED CASES OF JUDGE DEE (DEE GOONG AN), translated by Robert Van Gulik. Authentic 18th-century Chinese detective novel; Dee and associates solve three interlocked cases. Led to Van Gulik's own stories with same characters. Extensive introduction. 9 illustrations. 237pp. 5⅜ × 8½.
23337-5 Pa. $4.95

*Prices subject to change without notice.*

Available at your book dealer or write for free catalog to Dept. GI, Dover Publications, Inc., 31 East 2nd St., Mineola, N.Y. 11501. Dover publishes more than 175 books each year on science, elementary and advanced mathematics, biology, music, art, literary history, social sciences and other areas.